# AMERICA'S
# BEST
# KEPT
# SECRET

# AMERICA'S BEST KEPT SECRET

## James L. Gagan
### *Founder, United Consumers Club®*
### with Robert L. Shook

**CB**
CONTEMPORARY
BOOKS
CHICAGO

**Library of Congress Cataloging-in-Publication Data**

Gagan, James L.
  America's best kept secret / James L. Gagan and
Robert L. Shook.
      p.    cm.
    ISBN 0-8092-3976-0 (cloth)
        0-8092-3750-4 (paper)
      1. United Consumers Club (U.S.)—History.    2. Consumer
cooperatives—United States—History.    I. Shook, Robert L.
II. Title.
    HD3284.G34    1991
    334'.5'0973—dc20                                              91-12068
                                                                    CIP

Copyright © 1991 by James L. Gagan and Robert L. Shook
All rights reserved
Published by Contemporary Books, Inc.
180 North Michigan Avenue, Chicago, Illinois 60601
Manufactured in the United States of America
International Standard Book Number: 0-8092-3976-0 (cloth)
                                    0-8092-3750-4 (paper)

This book is dedicated to wife Claire,
sons Jack and Jim, and daughter Sarah.
Without you guys, nothing happens.

# CONTENTS

# ACKNOWLEDGMENTS

RECENTLY A POPULAR SONG included the refrain, "You are the wind beneath my wings" . . .

. . . I want to thank my collaborator, Bob Shook, whose discipline and talent have helped so much . . .

. . . and my publisher, Harvey Plotnick, and editor, Linda Gray—thanks again . . .

. . . and my best friends, Fred Wittlinger and Jack Allen, without whom I might have changed direction so many times, and who are the true heart and soul of UCC® . . .

. . . and thanks for the memory of my good friend and attorney, Byron Chudom—who always argued—seldom agreed with—but consistently supported me—God bless and keep you . . .

. . . and Gene Deutsch, the only accountant I've ever trusted, who has turned out to be so much more than just another "bean counter" . . .

. . . and my special friend, Ted Tannebaum, who taught me so much, especially that where there is love, there is life, and who continues to advise . . .

. . . and my "other wife," my "office wife," Armina Thorpe, for always being there . . .

. . . and the rest of the UCC® family who've made our success happen . . .

. . . and, most important, I want to thank God—Who has always blessed me beyond all imagination, for what reason I have never fully understood.

Jim Gagan
Palm Desert, California
March 10, 1991

# AMERICA'S
# BEST
# KEPT
# SECRET

# INTRODUCTION

IN THE AUTUMN OF 1971, I founded one of the most unusual businesses in America. My company, United Consumers Club®, is unusual because it sells practically everything and it doesn't advertise. It generates hundreds of millions of dollars in sales, yet it doesn't make a profit on the sale of merchandise. Still, it has a very healthy bottom line.

As this book goes to print, we're celebrating our twentieth anniversary, yet until you picked up this book, you probably had never heard of UCC®. So far, that's been by design. We've purposely maintained a low profile, and that's why the people who do business with us say we're the best-kept secret in America.

I'll let you in on another secret. The writing of this book marks the first time I have ever revealed the secrets to which I attribute my success. And by most people's standards, I am considered today to be a very successful man. My story is indeed one of rags to riches, and I'm sure my humble beginnings had a lot to do with why I have been so close-mouthed for so many years. Being poor during my youth has undoubtedly left me a bit paranoid about letting other people in on what I did. I didn't want to reveal my secrets for success because I didn't want to encourage or, for that matter, strengthen the competition.

Well, twenty years later and with a head of gray hair, I've overcome those fears, and I'll now tell my story. Besides, I now have such a running head start that by the time anyone can possibly catch up, I'll be too old to care. It's like that Rudyard Kipling poem, "The *Mary Gloster*," in which he wrote, "They copied all they could follow, but they couldn't copy my mind,/And I left 'em sweating and stealing, a year and a half behind."

It's a safe bet to say that my company is not your run-of-the-mill business. But then neither am I your typical entrepreneur. In fact, a lot of people who knew me way back when thought I was the most improbable person to ever have my own business. As far as they were concerned, I didn't have the background or the credentials to start a company, let alone to someday head a national organization. They didn't think there was a snowball's chance in hell that my off-the-wall concept would fly. Mark Twain could have had me in mind when he defined a crank as "a man with a new idea until it succeeds."

I have no quarrel that anyone might have picked me as the "least likely to succeed" in the class of 1949. The fact is they *couldn't* have picked me, because I dropped out of high school. I never had the advantage of being taught what they teach at the Harvard Business School or, for that matter, at any business school. The knowledge I have acquired over the years has come through experience—hands-on learning that some of the current crop of management gurus lack, but without which a lot is lost.

Don't get the wrong idea; I'm not knocking a formal education. A good education is a necessity today, and I pity the guy in today's competitive world who doesn't have one. There have been many times I wished I had the security and prestige that go with a formal education and a degree. But I have never been bitter about my lack of it, nor have I resented anyone who had one.

Today, I consider myself an educated man, and a lot of what I learned doesn't come from textbooks and isn't taught in any school. You just can't pick it up in the training program of a Fortune 500 company. As a consequence, some people think I'm a maverick because I don't do things by the book. But if I did, it would be redundant for me to write my own book on management style.

I must warn you, it's a style that works for me; it's not for everybody. Still, I'm delighted to share it with you. My advice is that you should pick and choose what will work best for you.

I will tell you up front that today's business climate is ultracompetitive. The risks are greater than ever. But so are the rewards for those who do succeed. What it boils down to is that there is little margin for error. In telling my story, I'll reveal many of my secrets that have never been told before—some of America's best-kept secrets that will provide you with an edge, help you to minimize your risk, and allow you to achieve the success you desire.

# —1—

# SUCCEEDING AGAINST THE ODDS

THE GRAVEYARD IS FILLED with would-be entrepreneurs. There are countless numbers of men and women who had a vision of building a successful business but whose dreams turned into financial nightmares.

In the American automobile industry, for example, only three automakers—General Motors, Ford, and Chrysler— remain. Yet as many as 300 U.S. companies have attempted to manufacture cars. In 1903, when Henry Ford started his company, no fewer than fifty-six other automakers also made their entry that very year. Over the years, the list of those that failed includes such notable names as Stutz, De Soto, Packard, Studebaker, Tucker, and the most recent automaker to go belly-up, the DeLorean Motor Company.

Granted that the rate of survival is higher in less capital-intensive industries, the vast majority of entrepreneurs do just that—they survive. Now, survival by itself does not represent much in the way of achievement. Yet the vast majority of small-business people accomplish little else—they drift aimlessly, and they create nothing more than what amounts to their own employment and perhaps a job here and there for a handful of others. Sadly, they operate mom-and-pop shops demanding extraordinarily long work hours, and unlike employees of large corporations, these self-employed people are often inadequately covered by health insurance and retirement plans. And though they are constantly subjected to the risk of losing everything they own, their annual earnings average no more than those of the millions of workers who put in their forty-hour week at a factory. Yet, unlike the worker, these people take home every disappointment and headache from the job at night. In essence, they're on call around the clock, 365 days a year. These are America's "independent" businessmen and -women. This is independence? Not in my book! In truth, these people are slaves to their businesses.

It is true that at the start of a new business venture, the owner's survival—to provide shelter, food, and clothing for his or her family—receives the highest priority. But there must be something more. There must be a dream—one with a realistic objective. Perhaps, at first, it's the attainment of a series of small goals—something that provides a sense of direction. Your sights must be set on where you want to be sometime in the distant future. Without such a mark, you will shoot randomly in the dark, leaving only to chance that you will hit your target. When so, the odds of success are indeed minimal.

My purpose in writing this book is to impart a message to those entrepreneurs who have a desire to build something more—something substantial. I want to address men and women who want to make a difference in this world. If you are one of these individuals, I can make a difference in your life. My objective is to show you not only how to survive, but how to succeed.

## In Search of a Concept

I can't pinpoint an exact moment when I came up with the United Consumers Club concept. A burning bush didn't appear in the wilderness, nor did a light bulb flash above my head in the middle of the night. (I would have liked that, because it would have provided me with a dramatic beginning for this book!) No, at that point in my life, my career had gone up and down like a roller coaster. I had had my share of hard knocks, and I had also enjoyed some prosperous times. In the summer of 1971, I was frustrated because even though I had achieved some success along the way, I had nothing to show for it. I badly wanted to find something I could sink my teeth into—something that I could enjoy doing for the rest of my life. My problem was that I didn't know what it would be. I just had to keep searching.

It's no easy matter to come up with a new idea. After all, since the beginning of time, this earth has been inhabited by billions of people who, in turn, have had trillions of ideas. Just thinking about such large numbers is mind-boggling. Each night I'd go to bed and lie there thinking, "What can I do that nobody else has ever done before?" It's funny, but when you try so hard to think, that's when you're least likely to come up with a creative thought. "All I need is just one idea," I kept saying to myself, ". . . only a single idea . . ."

There's an endless number of ideas out there. You just have to find one, and when you do, you must work it to death. Sometimes you have to explore dozens of opportunities, analyze them, and then take something from this one, something else from that one, and so on, until a brand-new concept evolves. While I didn't know it at the time, that's exactly what I did.

In my search for an exciting opportunity, I came across some direct-sales companies that, at the time, were going like gangbusters. One in particular was an Orlando-based cosmetics firm. Its founder had built an enormous pyramid sales organization that claimed it provided tremendous opportunities to amass a sizable fortune. I investigated the company and concluded that the firm's pie-in-the-sky promises were impossible dreams. I calculated that if each new distributor signed up other recruits according to the founder's quotas, by the end of the eighth round, the first-level distributor would have the entire population of the world working under him!

While pyramid sales organizations are no longer legal in the United States, this firm was a forerunner of the multilevel sales companies that are prevalent today. I checked a few out and even attended some distributors' meetings that turned out to be nothing more than pep rallies and sales pitches to recruit distributors to hire still other distributors. The sale of product was the last thing on their minds. They were in the business of selling distributorships, not merchandise. It was a real turnoff, but I did get a kick out of the "revival" aspect of these so-called business meetings. To me, it was enlightening to see so many people get so enthusiastic about a concept. If the top honchos had given the command to walk on water, I'm sure the nonswimmers would have drowned trying.

About the same time, coincidentally, a representative from a fraternal organization came to my home one evening to greet me, bearing what he declared was good news. "Congratulations, Mr. Gagan. You have been nominated to join our organization." It turned out the man was selling insurance. Although I didn't buy the insurance, he had an effective way to get me to listen to his presentation.

I continued looking at scores of business opportunities, many of which, on the surface, seemed promising, but upon closer scrutiny had only sizzle but no substance. I traveled all over the country, and once, on a whim, I went to Milwaukee to meet a man who operated a buyers' club. He wanted me to join his business and do in Indiana what he was doing in Wisconsin. He explained to me how, back in the 1950s and 1960s, he made a killing in the frozen-food-and-freezer business. "We'd sell the freezers at exorbitant prices, and then we'd sell 'em frozen food every month at outrageous prices to put in their freezers. And we let them finance the whole kit and caboodle, but naturally at loan shark rates," he boasted. "We made money by the barrel until legislation regulating the freezer business was passed. We were nailed on that one and got shut down. So I formed a buyers' club, and if ever I saw a potential money machine, this is it."

"Buyers' club?" I inquired. "Money machine?"

"Yeah, we sell people a membership to our club that permits them to buy merchandise from a handful of furniture firms at the manufacturer's cost—without any markup."

"Go on," I said, starting to get interested.

"For instance, a table might retail for $600, and we buy it for $300. So we show the member that the actual cost is $400, and we pocket a hundred bucks on the deal."

"But if you're making your money on the membership fee, why don't you sell it for what you said you would?" I asked. "At your cost."

"What for? Besides, they don't know the difference," he insisted.

"I'm not so sure about that," I replied. "And if you'd go ahead and deliver on your promise to provide a real bargain, the members would bring in their friends and relatives. I'd think that in the long run, you'd make even more money. What's more, you'd be able to sleep at night."

"I never have any problem sleeping," he answered. I believed him because it was evident that the man didn't have a conscience.

"I'll pass," I replied and headed toward the door.

### Identifying a Need and Filling It

It's one thing to want to start a business, but quite another to fill a need. If a need doesn't exist for your product or service, there's not much point in going into a particular field simply because you want to be in it. I've observed many would-be entrepreneurs who opened everything from restaurants to real estate agencies in areas already overcrowded with competition. They failed because they didn't fill a need.

At the time I was looking for something to do, I did quite a bit of soul-searching. I was living off my savings, and I was very concerned about how much was going out every month with nothing coming in. It would be only a matter of time before the proverbial well would run dry. I was putting my family in jeopardy, and it gave me an uneasy feeling. To make matters worse, the country was starting to feel the effects of inflation. Americans were beginning to express their anger over the shrinking dollar in their wallets; their purchasing power was slowly disappearing. Inflation was supposed to be something that wrecked the economies of other countries, but not America! Yet government reports were coming out that the value of the dollar was deteriorating at an unacceptable pace. In 1971, for example, a consumer needed to pay 121.3 cents for what had cost a dollar in 1967. That summer, on August 15, President Richard Nixon made a surprise announcement that he was invoking an immediate ninety-day freeze on wages, rents, and prices, the first such freeze since 1951, when the Truman Administration imposed such a ceiling to cope with the inflationary spiral generated during the first six months of the Korean War.

Nixon's harsh measures made Americans acutely aware that their paychecks were quickly eroding and that the result would be a significant decline in their standard of living. It was clearly a time for belt-tightening. As a middle-aged family man in need of work, I had my share of sleepless nights, consumed with worry about having my limited savings wiped out. I felt only a heartbeat away from losing what little I had accumulated to achieve a certain level of middle-class comfort. My worst nightmare was the possibility that my family would suffer. My concern about my own financial insecurity provided me with an awareness that millions of other Americans also were in the same boat and shared similar sinking feelings.

By putting the pieces of the puzzle together, I came up with the concept for United Consumers Club. The pieces included my own fears, which instilled me with an acute awareness about how millions of Americans shared a common frustration that resulted from a reduction in their discretionary spending. This translated into a diminished standard of living. Then there was the former frozen-food-and-freezer promoter who tried to sign me up for his buyers' club. Before that, it was the membership approach to buy an insurance policy. And during this time, thoughts about operating a large national direct-sales organization raced through my mind. To attract high-quality people who would share my commitment—to create a company with real substance, not just hype!

All during this time, I kept thinking about how inflation was hanging over every American's head like a black cloud. Thoughts about how we could deal with it kept hounding me. Then I noticed the purchasing power exhibited by business purchasing agents and agricultural co-ops. It occurred to me that if these groups were able to use their collective buying power to buy everything from paper clips and copy paper to combines and barbed wire in gross lots and realize a substantial savings, why couldn't a group of consumers do the same? Wouldn't it be wonderful if consumers could buy such things as furniture, carpeting, appliances—everything—at true wholesale prices because they had purchasing power?

At first, I figured all that would be necessary was to call a dozen friends, and we would buy perhaps a television set or a dining room set from a particular manufacturer at a wholesale price. But what were the odds of finding twelve other families who wanted to purchase an identical product at the exact same time I wanted to buy mine? Then I thought about talking to dozens of families and making a wish list of what they wanted, and when I accumulated enough items that coincided with enough other lists, we'd approach a manufacturer and place a large order. But who would be willing to wait so long? It took that trip to Milwaukee to provide me with the concept that would tie everything together.

The first tangible thing I did was to set down my thoughts on a legal-size pad of paper. They were: (1) Provide merchandise at truly wholesale prices; (2) Offer this merchandise to members only; and (3) Build a national sales organization. It was just three notes jotted down on a piece of paper. *It was a beginning.*

## Sell the Concept

People buy concepts, not products. For example, when an IBM sales rep walks into a prospect's office, the sales rep doesn't sell a little blue box, or whatever color a computer is. Instead, he or she tells a business owner, "I've got something that's going to make your job easier, reduce your cost, and allow you to give better service to your customers."

Other office equipment manufacturers sell concepts, too. Word processor and fax machine companies offer products that make crisp images in addition to saving time, providing convenience, and making work more efficient. Insurance companies don't sell complicated, legalistic documents, which, in fact, are what insurance policies are. Instead, they sell such things as security, peace of mind, and solutions to estate tax problems. Likewise, realtors don't sell bricks and mortar, automobile salespeople don't sell steel and wheels, travel agents don't sell tickets and reservations, and so on. *Nor does my company, UCC, sell plastic membership cards.*

Prior to forming the *business*, therefore, I wanted to see how people would react to the *concept*. So I said to them, "Suppose that you had many uncles who owned dozens of businesses. One was in the furniture business, another in home appliances, another in sporting goods, and many more. And each of these uncles agreed to sell you practically anything you wanted at his exact cost."

"Yeah, it would be terrific, wouldn't it, Jim? That's a nice dream."

It was with this dream that I made the decision to start a business that provided a service of this nature. My company would be everyone's uncle! My plan was to approach manufacturers and inform them that my company would serve as an organization to offer their merchandise directly to certain consumers but with no profits from these sales. It would eliminate all middlemen. The manufacturer would still receive its normal profit.

By working through many manufacturers, I'd be many uncles to many people. So what was in it for me? Notice that I previously referred to this venture as a business, and a business must generate a profit in order to survive. If I wasn't going to make anything on the sale of merchandise, how could my business exist? My idea included charging a fee to provide this service. The revenues from these fees would generate the company's profit.

In October 1971, I incorporated United Consumers Club,

Inc., an organization with members who pay dues entitling them to buy at true wholesale prices. A membership provides the right to make purchases through manufacturers' and suppliers' catalogs in a UCC showroom—the catalogs are the same that retailers use when they buy and include the exact suggested retail and/or wholesale price lists. Without the overhead that it takes to operate a retail business, we can make our money strictly from membership fees. Obviously, the fee must be low enough, or it would negate the savings offered on the cost of merchandise. If that were the case, there'd be no reason for our existence.

## Refining the Concept

I was convinced there was a definite need for an entity such as UCC, and it appeared that people would be receptive to it. In short, UCC would enable the average consumer to cut costs and battle inflation. While nobody could argue with me about that, at the time, my relatives and friends thought that while it was a noble ambition, it was also an impossible dream.

"How are you going to sign up manufacturers to sell their products to your members at wholesale prices?" they asked.

"With large numbers of members," I explained, "the club will have enough clout so manufacturers will look at us as a large buying organization. Besides, they're interested in volume, not in what the consumer pays."

"Why would anyone be willing to pay a fee to buy merchandise? There's no fee charged to buy retail," they scoffed.

"Oh, yes, there is," I insisted. "Every time you buy retail, you pay a markup, the gross profit on the item you purchase. Those tariffs add up to be many more times than the fee that my members will pay for joining my club."

Others pointed out that the vast majority of people would be too skeptical to shell out fees to belong to my club. I was aware of how the American consumer had been bombarded for years with so-called new types of retailing concepts. They had been hit with everything from the warehouse-type discount retailers to television shopping channels. And they had been through the mill with such unscrupulous sales tactics as the bait and switch, loss leaders, highball and lowball sales pitches, and phony going-out-of-business sales. I knew it was going to be an uphill battle, but I also knew that my basic premise was good because it filled a real void in the marketplace. I understood there would be obstacles along the way, but then what pioneer hasn't met with resistance? (As it turned out, I underestimated the hurdles I would face. No matter how good a new product or service may be, you can't even give it away to the doubting Thomases.)

Like all clubs, UCC had to establish certain rules. To protect the manufacturers, I decided that the club would not advertise, nor would members be allowed to divulge confidential price information. Another rule was that members were not permitted to purchase items from the club and resell the goods. Furthermore, members were only permitted to buy for themselves and their families, the only exception being when purchasing gifts.

Setting up UCC as a club had several advantages. Although it is a business, I believed that, as members, people would be instilled with pride resulting from the sense of belonging to something. In turn, this pride would make them more aware of the importance of following the club's rules. As members, they would feel comfortable nominating relatives and friends to join. Also, a club theme presented a warm and less threatening atmosphere. Finally, in a club, members could more easily accept the fact that UCC's source of profit comes solely from the membership fees, not from the sale of merchandise.

## A Revolution in the Marketplace

What marketing system could be better than one in which manufacturers sell directly to consumers? Eliminating what can amount to several layers of distribution enables the consumer to buy at the lowest possible price. It also means that if the buyer chooses to spend the same amount of money for merchandise sold at retail, he or she can afford to purchase a higher-quality product. This has its benefits, too. It means additional pleasure, less service required, and less waste because of greater durability.

To my knowledge, nobody has ever been able to devise a way to provide more value to the buyer through the standard channels of distribution. It stands to reason that cutting out middlemen lowers the price of merchandise. There is one fallacy. When a consumer buys a single unit directly from the manufacturer, the maker has extra costs compared to when it sells large quantities to a single retail buyer. As a buying club, however, UCC is able to place multiple orders at a time, and, in turn, the merchandise is forwarded directly to each club. This procedure requires only a single account to be set up with each supplier, reducing various costs normally incurred for establishing credit, billing, bookkeeping, and so on.

There are no utopias in this world. This marketing system has a few drawbacks. UCC members buy merchandise from catalogs, so it's possible for something to be ordered that "doesn't look like it did in the photograph." There is also a waiting period before the merchandise is delivered, and when it arrives, it must be picked up at the club. To most people, this is a small sacrifice, especially when buying wholesale at such tremendous savings.

### Ideas Are a Dime a Dozen, but the Men and Women Who Implement Them Are Priceless

During the past twenty years, I've had hundreds of men and women ask me for advice on new business ventures they had in mind. While many were potentially good ideas, only a handful were ever implemented. That's why I say, "Ideas are a dime a dozen, but the men and women who implement them are priceless." There's a big difference between talking about starting a business and actually putting your money where your mouth is and executing your game plan.

Of course, once you have an idea, you must know what to do with it. For example, somebody could think of a wonderful plot for a novel or a movie, but without the writing talent to produce a manuscript or a screenplay, the story idea by itself is of little value. I've daydreamed about many such stories I thought would make great movies. But without my doing anything about them, that's just what they were—daydreams.

I remember the hot Pet Rock fad back in 1975, when millions of people were shelling out four bucks to buy an oval-shaped sand rock that was worth less than a penny. The rock was packaged in a box with some air holes in the lid to allow the rock to breathe, and it came with a small instruction manual giving directions on "how to train your new pet." Countless Americans were saying, "Why didn't I think of an idea like that? I could have made millions!" Even if they had had such an idea, however, few would have known what to do with it. Gary Dahl, the father of the pet rock, did know. He knew how to write the clever copy that appeared in the manual and on the box, how to generate national publicity to be featured on national talk shows including "The Tonight Show" and in magazines such as *Newsweek*, how to establish quick and efficient distribution, and so on. Without the implementation, the Pet Rock would have bombed, and instead of calling Dahl a genius, people would have said he had rocks in his head.

Now let's get back to my concept of a revolutionary marketing system. It is true that I had a unique concept, but until I followed through with its implementation, it was just one of those dime-a-dozen ideas. While UCC members and their families today are nearly a half million strong, and we now have more than five hundred suppliers, back in 1971 there were zero members and zero suppliers. To today's casual observer, UCC is such a logical concept. With our huge buying power, suppliers are eager to make their goods available to our members, and with so many manufacturers, with their tens of thousands of products to sell at wholesale prices, consumers consider us an attractive alternative to buying retail. As you can imagine, however, twenty years ago it took a lot of selling to convince a manufacturer to be a UCC supplier—because when we first started, there were no members in the club. Likewise, there wasn't much incentive to be a member when there were no suppliers. At the very beginning, I was faced with the age-old story about which came first, the chicken or the egg. Or, in my case, suppliers or members.

I made the decision to first line up some suppliers, resolving that only afterward would I attempt to sell memberships. I knew it would be a monumental sales job to have people purchase memberships, and it would be a disaster if they came to a showroom with no catalogs from which to purchase merchandise. What's more, I didn't want to build a reputation for ripping off people, and if UCC didn't have a reasonable number of suppliers, my business would have been just that—one gigantic rip-off.

Just after Byron Chudom, a dynamic young man who was both my attorney and a close personal confidant, had incorporated UCC, he told me about a young, dynamic sales rep, Fred Wittlinger, who sold IBM equipment to him. "I think the world of Fred," Byron said, "and if you can get him, he'd be terrific. Fred is the entrepreneurial type, and he's always talking about starting a business of his own someday. But he's doing well with IBM, so if he could do this on the side until it takes off . . . "

"No problem," I replied. "Fred can start a franchise with me, and once it's going, he can hire a manager to operate it."

My office was in my home in Merrillville, Indiana, and that's where Fred and I first met. I put together a rather primitive presentation about the UCC concept that consisted of a three-ring binder with some photocopies of some products and a price page that I was able to obtain from a manufacturer's catalog. Fred listened intently, asked a few questions, and let me do most of the talking. I told him that I planned to franchise my business and mentioned that he could purchase one in his hometown, Valparaiso, Indiana, a town with a population of twenty thousand, located twenty miles east of my home. I wasn't sure he had any interest whatsoever, so after about an hour, I asked, "What do you think about this?"

"I've never seen anything like it," he said in a soft voice.

"But do you like it?" I asked, holding my breath.

"It's phenomenal!"

Boy, did I feel good when I heard that!

"I'd like to take this information home and discuss it with my wife, Jane," he said.

"Of course," I replied. "And, here, let me give you a franchise agreement that Byron made up for me. It's one that we modeled after studying the twenty-five top franchising companies in the world. Take this home and show it to your wife and, may I suggest, your attorney and accountant."

"Great, I'll run it by Jack Allen, a close friend and a college fraternity brother who practices law in Valparaiso."

A few days later, Fred called me and asked if he could bring Jack by to meet me. The three of us chatted for about an hour, and Jack said, "Let me run this by my wife, Jody, and if she likes it as much as Jane did, the four of us will buy the Valparaiso franchise."

Jody was as excited as the other three, so the two couples made an oral commitment to start a club together sometime after the first of the year. By then, the Christmas holidays were in full swing, and everything came to a standstill. For the last few weeks of 1971, I mulled over the necessity of lining up some suppliers, and in a hurry. Until I did, UCC was only a dream, not a business. It dawned on me that the best place to meet with large numbers of manufacturers was at the Furniture Mart in Chicago, where the major furniture firms housed large, fancy showrooms and gathered twice a year to introduce their new lines to thousands of buyers in the retail field. (In later years, the Furniture Mart would be absorbed by the Merchandise Mart.) I figured that big-ticket items like dining room sets and bedroom sets would be the ideal type of merchandise to offer through the club. All a member would have to do was make a single purchase, and he or she would save several times the cost of the membership. The next showing at the mart was scheduled in early January, about an hour's drive from my home, and there they'd be—all lined up like ducks in a row, waiting to sell their goods through UCC—or so I thought.

I marked January 6, 1972, on my calendar as the day I'd visit the Furniture Mart, a huge seventeen-story building, which at the time was the nation's largest furniture showplace. As far as everyone in the industry was concerned, the mart was the center of the world, the place where every major manufacturer sold its merchandise to the retailers who made the pilgrimage to Chicago. Fred Wittlinger, who was still true-blue to IBM and had not yet started the Valparaiso club, would join me on the trip.

## Nothing Happens Until Something Is Sold

I remember reading about the difficult times NCR salespeople had selling the first cash registers. "What do I need that contraption for?" angry retailers said. "I just keep my money in a drawer. My employees will think I don't trust them if I have to ring up sales in that thing. And besides, it's just an unnecessary expense to add to my overhead."

While it would be hard to find a retailer who does not have a cash register today, like most other products, it had to be sold. My first UCC franchise sale to Jack and Fred was a piece of cake. But I can assure you, there were many tough sales that followed. In particular, it took a lot of selling to line up our first suppliers. If I couldn't sell manufacturers on my UCC concept, that first franchise scheduled to open in Valparaiso wouldn't have been worth a hill of beans.

When Fred and I arrived at the Furniture Mart, there were tens of thousands of buyers from around the United States and abroad who were also there, and they had something we didn't have—preregistration passes. Those without a pass had to wait in long registration lines, and only upon properly identifying themselves were given one.

Fred and I stood in the line. About fifteen minutes later, we finally came face-to-face with the lady at the registration table. "Your company name, please?" she asked.

"United Consumers Club," I casually replied, as if I fully expected it to be on her list.

She looked through some papers and said, "I'm sorry, but I can't find it."

"Keep on looking," I said, as if it would show up.

No matter how much she searched, it wasn't there, which, of course, was no surprise to me. Nonetheless, I acted indignant.

"We're a new company. Perhaps it's listed with the new companies."

"How long have you been in business?"

"That's none of your business," I said in a huff.

"Who are your suppliers that you're planning to visit?" she asked.

"I don't reveal that kind of information."

"I'm sorry, but . . ."

"Look, ma'am, I know you have a job to do," I interrupted, "and so do I. Now I suggest that you give Mr. Wittlinger and me a pass right this moment, and if not, here's what's going to happen. We're not going to attend the mart, and that means I won't see my suppliers. And do you know what? They're going to be very upset, and I'm going to tell them exactly what happened just now. Now you'll save everybody a lot of grief, including yourself, if you'll just give us our passes. And that shouldn't be so difficult. After all, the manufacturers are here to sell furniture, and we've come to buy furniture. Furthermore, it's not your job to discourage the sale of furniture."

With that, she shuffled through some papers and said, "Oh, yes, I've found your name. It was spelled incorrectly. Please spell your names for me so I can type up passes."

Naturally, this was her way to save face, which was fine with me. "G-A-G-A-N, and W-I-T-T-L-I-N-G-E-R," I enunciated very slowly.

"Here are your passes, sir."

"That was a relief," I thought to myself, and I chalked up another sale in my mind.

We spent several hours wandering the halls, going in and out of manufacturers' showrooms, getting the feel of the land. Eventually we approached our first manufacturer. That first encounter was a real eye-opener, particularly when the time came for me to answer some questions in order to open an account.

The man took out an application, and I knew I was in trouble as soon as I gave him my business address, which was the same as my home address.

"Exactly what is United Consumers Club, Mr. Gagan?"

I knew I wasn't helping my cause when I started to explain the concept.

"How many members belong to the club?"

"Er, only a few right now, but we're going to have a lot someday," I muttered. "We're going to start working on that as soon as we get the merchandise."

"You know we wouldn't dare allow you to advertise that you're selling at our cost. Why, you'd wreck our distribution."

"We don't intend to advertise," I replied.

"It doesn't matter; we can't sell our merchandise to you at wholesale prices anyhow," the man fired back. "You're not a retailer, and we only sell to retailers. You shouldn't be here at the mart in the first place."

Fred and I walked out in a huff, visited a few more furniture houses, and for the rest of the day, we got shot down, over and over again.

It was a long drive back to Merrillville that night, and while Fred was obviously a little down, I wasn't about to let him know I was, too. "OK, Fred," I said, trying to encourage him, "we didn't do so well our first day out. But there are still four days left before the end of the mart. We have to regroup, and then we're going to hit 'em again tomorrow."


## Breaking the Ice

In the beginning it's always exceedingly difficult to sell a new concept. It's hard to break the ice, but once you do, the selling gets easier. Most people don't want to be the first ones. It's mainly because they don't believe a revolutionary idea will ever get off the ground. Until they see some success, they stand back on the sidelines with a wait-and-see attitude. Or worse, they ridicule it and tell you all the reasons why it can't work.

The following day when Fred and I went to the mart, I

came prepared. I anticipated resistance and came equipped with the right answers.

After introducing myself as the president of UCC, a national buying club, I was again asked, "How many members do you have?"

This time, instead of giving a direct answer, I fired back, "Are you a member of any particular club?"

"What do you mean?"

"It's a simple question," I said. "Do you belong to the Elks, the Masons, the Fraternal Order of Police, or perhaps a country club?"

"Er, yes, as a matter of fact, I do."

"Well then, I don't have to tell you that most private organizations don't publicize their membership, and *neither do we*. If anything is sacred to us, it's our membership. We don't sell lists, nor do we ever plan to do anything that might disturb our members. I am sure that you can appreciate why we can't divulge confidential information."

This rebuttal worked like a charm. Nobody pushed me any further about our numbers, which, of course, was a legitimate inquiry that's relevant to our buying power. Instead, they asked, "How does the club work?"

That was the opening I was waiting for. From there, I elaborated on the merits of belonging to our club and how it was a wonderful outlet for qualified furniture manufacturers that met our high standards. "Of course, you must understand that we don't advertise," I said up front, not allowing anyone to confront me with this issue.

UCC's first supplier was Burris Industries, a soft goods manufacturer that makes such things as sofas, chairs, and end tables. By the end of the mart, UCC had thirty suppliers. It was a wonderful week, and we were on our way. Now, all UCC needed was members.

# —2—

# WITH BLINDERS, YOU CAN SEE THE LIGHT AT THE END OF THE TUNNEL

A FLEDGLING ENTREPRENEUR must have a strong conviction; starting a business is not for the faint-hearted. There are a zillion things out there to throw you off track. For starters, there are well-meaning friends and relatives who will make every effort to convince you that your new venture won't work. They'll even go so far as to spell out why you have no right to even attempt it. This was especially true in my case, because the UCC concept was unorthodox. Then there are the usual handicaps, such as being underfinanced, fierce competition, long, back-breaking hours of work, and the insecurity of feeling your way in the dark.

I had my share of insecure moments, and so does every businessperson. Nobody ever said it would be easy. There are no sure things in the business arena when it comes to a new venture. The risk factor is always present and ominous. What makes my blood pressure rise is to see books that promise risk-free or effort-free wealth on bestseller lists. Nobody ever *earns* wealth without risk taking. The only ways I know to amass substantial sums of money without risk are by inheriting it, marrying it, or winning it in a lottery.

Entrepreneuring and risk taking are synonymous. Businesspeople must not allow themselves to entertain thoughts about eliminating all perils by playing it completely safe. To do so is tantamount to abandoning one's original goal and accepting mediocrity. Anyone who begins to concentrate on every conceivable way to avoid risk taking has lost focus on his or her initial objectives. If you're ever going to see the light at the end of the tunnel, you must wear blinders. You must not allow any distractions to destroy your dreams.

From the very beginning, I was determined that UCC would be a national company. I had no intention of opening a single club or, for that matter, a handful of clubs in Indiana or in the tri-state region (Indiana, Illinois, and Ohio). I firmly believed that a buying club could succeed only if it operated on a large scale. I understood that UCC's eventual success depended on having buying power that could only come with economy of scale. It was essential to achieve a certain size in order to attract major suppliers. To put it simply, if our membership was not extensive enough to generate large orders, suppliers would have little incentive to handle us as an account. Knowing this, I have made it a point to never deviate from my goal. UCC was founded on the premise that it would someday be a national organization. Nothing short of this objective would be acceptable.

## How Do You Eat an Elephant?

Have you heard the old riddle, How do you eat an elephant? The answer is *one bite at a time.* There's an important message here for every entrepreneur. While you must have a long-range game plan, you must also pay attention to short-term objectives. While my sights were set on building a national organization, however, I also concentrated on the mundane, day-to-day business at hand. Although I had visions of coast-to-coast UCC clubs, each club was opened one at a time.

I'm all for thinking big. Quite frankly, I can't imagine anyone starting a business venture and *not* wanting to have it grow as much as possible. It's not healthy, however, to have visions of grandeur, seeing only the big picture and neglecting what must be done on a daily basis. For instance, it's fine for an individual to open a hamburger stand and aspire to some-day having a chain of fast-food restaurants across the country. But the person shouldn't get so caught up with the ambition of operating a thousand outlets that he or she fails to devote the proper amount of attention to make operation number one succeed. Only when the first store is truly a success should the restaurant owner attempt to duplicate that effort with a second one. Even then, branch number one will require additional skills, because the entrepreneur must develop somebody else to operate it. Later, by repeating the success of the first store, the entrepreneur can open another and again another. Each opening demands his or her attention, because if the first ones go under—unless the owner regroups and figures out what went wrong—his or her long-term goal is only a pipe dream.

## You Don't Have to Be a Genius to Have a Million-Dollar Idea

There are very few geniuses in the world of business. And thank heavens, that's not what it takes to be a success! The vast majority of highly successful people I have met are, in fact, ordinary men and women who do extraordinarily well in a particular area where they developed a specific expertise. Then, by concentrating on what they do so well, they repeated the process and eventually made millions. This may sound like an oversimplification, and perhaps it is, but it's what generally happens.

To achieve success, you don't have to repeatedly come up with incredibly brilliant ideas in order to keep the momentum going. I don't think it's possible for the majority of entrepreneurs to be so innovative that they can continually come up with a steady flow of new concepts. It takes only a single idea; then you must work at it and continually refine it. And with the proper effort combined with perseverance, a fortune can be made.

I'll go one step further and state that it's not even necessary to have a *completely* original idea to produce a million-dollar winner. It is certainly acceptable to "borrow" from others, modify or expand an idea, and subsequently claim what evolves as your own. As Oliver Wendell Holmes said, "Many times ideas grow better when transplanted from one mind to another." Domino's Pizza is a shining example. Founder Tom Monaghan didn't invent pizza, but he made a fortune by merging two existing ideas into a new one. When Monaghan opened his first store in Ann Arbor, Michigan, in the early 1970s, the pizza industry was considered a saturated field. There were pizza parlors galore in every neighborhood across America, and the turnover was staggering. So what did Monaghan have to offer America that was different? Domino's *delivered* pizza. And what was so new and creative about delivering food? At the time, there were countless delivery services. Monaghan observed that pizza wasn't often delivered, because people like to eat it while it's still hot. It didn't take a genius to figure out a way for the pizza to still be hot when the Domino's delivery truck arrived. The technology already existed, so Monaghan didn't have to reinvent the wheel. His concept was simple: make good pizza and deliver hot pizza. He merely combined two existing ideas and, in the process, came up with an innovative new business, one that became a billion-dollar corporation.

When Fred Smith founded Federal Express Corp. in the early 1980s, he, too, refined an existing idea. After all, Federal Express is nothing more than a mail service—it does the same thing the postal system does with billions of letters and packages. Smith simply developed a way to provide guaranteed overnight delivery. It costs a lot more to send it Smith's way, but evidently Americans are willing to pay several times the rate charged by the United States Postal Service to make sure their letters arrive in twenty-four hours. So, you see, Fred Smith didn't actually develop an original concept, but in my book he's a highly innovative individual. What he did do was make a needed improvement on a service that every American adult has used thousands of times and something that is as old as civilization itself.

As much as I'd like to pat myself on the back and tell you

I'm a genius, I'm far from it. That's not what it took to start
UCC. It only required studying the marketing system that
had existed in this country for the past two hundred years. I
looked at it and figured out how to improve it. It was there for
everyone to analyze. I simply found a shortcut by which the
consumer can buy directly from the manufacturer. I fine-
tuned the marketing process by eliminating unnecessary distribution channels, so consumers who became UCC members
could realize tremendous savings. Certainly, manufacturers
had sold directly to the consumer in the past. If you go back
far enough, early people bartered—there were no middlemen.

Once you come up with your concept, the real secret is
having the gumption to stick with it and stay away from
anything that distracts you from your original game plan. In
my business, there were all sorts of distractions that could
have easily tempted me to deviate from my conceived design.
Once we were off and running, people approached me with
money-making deals that looked tempting, and although they
offered some attractive short-term gains, they would have
adversely affected UCC's long-term objectives. For instance,
suggestions poured in to sell food at discounted prices. The
thinking was that once we had the members, why not supply
them with what they eat, too? There were many products and
services to offer, but I resisted temptation and stuck to my
game plan. This is not to suggest that an entrepreneur should
avoid all new ideas and never be receptive to change. *There is
a big difference between being inflexible and wearing blinders.*

## You Don't Have to Reinvent the Wheel

At UCC, we're constantly asking our people to be innovative.
I'm convinced that if we ever stop looking for methods to
improve our business, we'll stop growing. We keep asking our
people for their ideas, and we regularly conduct brainstorm-
ing sessions for suggestions to fine-tune our modus operandi.
It is not, however, necessary to continually reinvent the wheel.
UCC is a buyers' club, and we have no intention of being in
another business.

While I had the good fortune to come up with a creative marketing concept, I don't let my ego get in my way and think of myself as some sort of a creative genius. I have no obsession to come up with a series of original thoughts and start up companies. Thomas Edison was a genius and one of the world's greatest inventors, with more than a thousand patents to prove it. I've never had a patent and doubt if I ever will. Fortunately, I don't have to have one. There is so much still to be achieved by UCC, I don't have to venture into uncharted waters that are unrelated to my own business. Until there are UCC clubs all over the country, we plan to concentrate on our own business and have no thoughts about entering other fields for expansion.

## The Flip Side of
## "Don't Put All Your Eggs in One Basket"

You've heard the old saying "don't put all your eggs in one basket." Well, I don't buy it. There's nothing wrong with putting all your eggs in one basket, but you'd better make damn sure you watch that basket. This is particularly true in today's fiercely competitive world. There are too many smart people out there making it too difficult to have expertise in more than one area.

In their bestselling book, *In Search of Excellence*, Tom Peters and Robert Waterman hammer home a "stick to the knitting" philosophy to which I strongly adhere. Throughout their book, they stress that successful corporations work hard at what they do best. While well-managed companies branch out, the ones that stick to the knitting generally outperform those that don't. Peters and Waterman emphasize that organizations that branch out into related fields also perform well, but this second group does not prosper to the extent of the first group. They claim, as a general rule, that companies that diversify into a wide variety of fields (in particular, those that make acquisitions of companies in unrelated industries) tend to wither on the vine.

Of course, there are good marriages in related industries.

The world's two largest automobile manufacturers, General Motors and Ford, own the world's number one and number two finance companies. They've succeeded in these ventures because their customers have a need to finance cars and trucks—so there's a natural tie-in. Likewise, it was a natural match for Budweiser to distribute peanuts and pretzels with its beer. The danger is when a company enters unrelated fields.

There are scores of corporations and individuals who were successful in a particular industry but met with failure when they diversified. Although Heublein had expertise in the wine and liquor industry, it didn't know beans about operating a chain of restaurants. Consequently, its Colonel Sanders acquisition was a calamity. In 1989, in a stick-to-the-knitting move, Coca-Cola, the world's number one soft-drink producer and distributor, sold its interests in Columbia Pictures Entertainment to Sony. And Robert Campeau, the Canadian billionaire who amassed a fortune in real estate, lost his entire fortune as a result of his takeover of Federated Department Stores.

The newspapers are full of stories about costly mistakes made by people a lot smarter than I who have gone astray from their original businesses. Their failures furnish powerful lessons, constantly reminding me to stick to the area in which I have made my mark. While UCC has prospered, we still have a long way to go before reaching our full potential. Knowing this, it would be foolish for us to divert our efforts by thinking we're so good that we should be engaged in an additional business.

## Beware of Doomsayers with Good Intentions

Thomas Carlyle once said, "Every new opinion, at its starting, is precisely in a minority of one." It's so true that when somebody has a new idea, there are hordes of people out there standing in line, anxious to tear it down.

I suppose anyone who has ever dared to do something

different had his or her share of doomsayers on hand to offer a few words of discouragement. When Alexander Graham Bell first tried to obtain financing for his new invention, he was told to remove "that toy" from the banker's office. (Fortunately for all of us, Bell took his telephone to another bank.) The esteemed Lord Kelvin, president of England's Royal Society from 1890 to 1895, was well respected for his scientific achievements. The people of England listened carefully when the lord made three brilliant predictions: radio has no future, heavier-than-air flying machines are impossible, and x-rays will prove to be a hoax. Later, Dr. Robert Millikan, a 1923 Nobel Prize winner, declared, "There is no likelihood man can ever tap the power of the atom," and, in 1948, Mary Somerville, a pioneer of radio educational broadcast, announced, "Television won't last. It's a flash in the pan."

When I began conceptualizing UCC's initial business plan, just about everyone I approached for feedback told me why it wouldn't work. "Nobody in his right mind is going to pay a membership fee so he can buy from a club," I was told. "You'll never be able to open accounts with manufacturers. Their existing accounts won't let them sell to you." "How are you going to sign up members when you don't have any suppliers lined up?" "How are you going to line up suppliers when you don't have any members?" Others simply said, "Jim, it's just not going to work."

"But why do you think it won't work?" I asked.

"It just won't. Take my word for it," I kept hearing.

One close friend went out of his way to stop by my house on a Saturday afternoon. "I just heard about that cockamamie idea of yours, Jim, and I wanted to warn you not to do it."

"I appreciate your concern," I started to say, but was interrupted. "I'm only here because I care about you and Claire and the kids, Jim. Now listen to me for your own sake. You're one helluva salesman, so if you want to sell something, sell life insurance. You'd be terrific at it. And it's an intangible just like your buyers' club idea. But life insurance is a proven thing—and everybody needs it. Now I want you to forget about that nonsense about starting a buyers' club, OK?"

In spite of well-meaning friends and relatives giving me every possible reason why I was destined to fail, I was determined to go ahead with it.

One mistake I made and highly advise any business pioneer to avoid was this: *don't call on your friends and relatives first.* I did because I believed so strongly in what I was selling and I wanted to share it with them. As a result, the first thirty sales presentations were made to friends and relatives, and I went zero for thirty. It was only when I started making calls on strangers that I was able to sell memberships. To rephrase a quote from the Bible, "A man is not a prophet in his hometown." The people who knew me looked at the club as a retail operation, and because I had no prior retailing or marketing experience, they didn't think I had any idea how to make it work. Strangers were receptive because they didn't know what my friends and relatives knew.

Luckily, I recalled how these same friends and relatives had tried to convince me that I shouldn't work for a collection agency because I came from a blue-collar family. "What right does a high school dropout like you have taking a job where you don't have to use your back?" they told me back then. Later, when I started my own collection agency, they hollered, "What? *You* want to be a business owner? Are you crazy? You don't know how to run a business. Be smart and work for somebody else. That way you're guaranteed a salary." And do you know what? I honestly think they thought they were giving me the right advice *for my own good*!

## The "Conditional No"

With all the nos I was getting, it was natural for me to have had some doubts about whether I'd ever get my idea off the ground. I'm only human and, with everyone telling me UCC didn't stand a chance, I began to think that maybe I could be wrong. Perhaps it was only because I so badly wanted it to work that I wasn't listening to what was indeed good advice. Then, too, when *everyone* was telling me not to do it, I began to wonder whether it was my stubborn streak driving me in the wrong direction. "Maybe," I thought, "I'm just trying to prove to everyone that I'm smart and that everyone else is wrong." That made me think, "If that's what's driving me, I am a dummy!" I also knew that my friends and relatives were on my side. They truly wanted what they *believed* was in my best interest. It's excruciatingly difficult to turn your back on advice given by the people who are rooting for you in this world.

The most discouraging times were when I sought advice from successful businesspeople whom I respected, and they, too, said the business couldn't work. Fortunately, early in the game, I was able to differentiate between *no* and the *conditional no*. The first no is a *simple no*. I'd run my UCC ideas past somebody, and he'd say, "No, Jim, I don't see it. It's not going to work." If I were to accept a simple opinion so matter-of-factly stated, I might have been convinced that I shouldn't start up my new business. However, I pressed people to tell me in detail why they didn't think it would work.

"Well, if you could really get manufacturers to sell to your members at the actual cost, that's a different story. Then even *I* would sign up. Who wouldn't? But you're never going to be able to get them, Jim."

I learned to read between the lines and not take these comments at face value. "What if I told you that the club would have fifty manufacturers?" I'd say.

"If you could do that, I'd be crazy not to sign up. But I don't believe you can do that. No one has ever done it before, so how are you going to do it? Besides, you know nothing about the retail business."

In spite of all the reasons why they'd say it wouldn't work, I was able to extract a conditional no out of them. "Well, yeah, *if you could do that* . . . sure I'd join." I interpreted this to mean that the UCC concept was actually a good one. However, they didn't think it could be implemented or, if it could, not by me. I could accept that. First, because it had never been done before, and people almost always reject the unproven. Second, I didn't have the background to lend credibility to my proposal, so why should anyone have any confidence in me? The important thing was for me to believe I could do it. That's what really mattered.

## Sounding Boards

I strongly recommend that you stay away from doomsayers who thrive on forecasting your imminent failure. Instead, surround yourself with bright, positive people who are not only rooting for you but can provide valuable feedback that can contribute to your ultimate success.

Frankly, I don't like being in the company of people who think negatively. And nothing is more negative and annoying than to have so-called friends constantly telling me what I am doing wrong or that it's only a matter of time before my business goes belly-up. Although I initially didn't conscientiously seek them out this way, my friends and associates outside my business have always been successful, intelligent individuals who provided me with positive reinforcement. In retrospect, I suppose I've always been attracted to this type; I'm just naturally turned off by negative people. But knowing what I know today, I'd advise anyone starting a new venture to be selective about whom he or she hangs out with—outsiders can be positive or negative, and they do have an influence on one's thinking.

Over the years, my support team included a cross-section of advisors consisting of leading businesspeople, CPAs, and, yes, attorneys. Speaking of attorneys, it was Shakespeare who wrote, "The first thing we do, let's kill all the lawyers," and it was my good friend and attorney Paul Giorgi who added the punchline: "but first let's be sure to get good counsel." Frankly, there are some matters on which I don't make a move without consulting my legal counsel and accountants. In today's complex world, so many business decisions involve getting the right legal and taxation opinions. Consequently, any businessperson who doesn't is operating in the dark and looking for trouble. Over the years, I've concluded that getting cheap accountants and lawyers is absolutely the wrong place to attempt to cut back on expenses.

One of my closest confidants is Ted Tannenbaum, a man I met by chance back in 1975 at a Las Vegas golf outing held by the Board of Trade and Mercantile Exchange. By fate, Ted and I were teamed in a foursome, and by the end of the round we had become the best of friends. Although Ted has a law degree, he's a very successful Chicago entrepreneur who knows a lot of top people, and through him I made some excellent contacts in the financial world. But most importantly, ever since our first meeting, Ted has been a tremendous sounding board, which has meant so much to me.

This brings up another subject. I strongly recommend every corporation have several outside board members. I feel it's a serious mistake for a board of directors to consist only of inside people. It's imperative to get bright individuals from a cross-section of different backgrounds who can offer a broader perspective. It's too easy for myopia to settle in when there's no diversity in the selection of board members. Big corporations such as General Motors, Ford, Citicorp, and IBM have outside board members, and small, privately owned corporations should do the same.

## The Critics

Fortunately, I wasn't the first person to receive criticism. To show you how wrong people can be about a concept, take a look at some comments about what the critics had to say about some of the world's most creative people:

> "Shakespeare's name, you may depend on it, stands absurdly too high and will go down."
> —Lord Byron, 1814

> "This is a book for the season only."
> —from the *New York Herald Tribune*'s review of
> F. Scott Fitzgerald's *The Great Gatsby*

"I'm sorry, Mr. Kipling, but you just don't know how to use the English language."
          —a rejection letter from the *San Francisco Examiner* to Rudyard Kipling in 1889

"Strauss can be characterized in four words: little talent, much impudence."
          —Cesar Cui, December 5, 1904

"Brahms evidently lacks the breadth and power of invention eminently necessary for the production of truly great symphonic work."
          —*Musical Courier*, New York, 1887

"Sure-fire rubbish."
          —from a review in the *New York Herald Tribune* of George Gershwin's *Porgy and Bess* in 1935

"The Beatles? They are on the wane."
          —The Duke of Edinburgh, 1965

Richard Bach's *Jonathan Livingston Seagull* was rejected by more than twenty publishers. "Look, they're not interested in a talking seagull," his agent told him. Macmillan Publishers finally accepted it, and the book sold one million hardback copies and many millions in its paperback editions.

Obviously, the critics can be wrong. When the critics come down on me with harsh comments, I like to read the following quote:

"It is not the critic who counts, not the man who points out how the strong man stumbles or where the doer of deeds could have done them better. The credit belongs to the man who is actually in the arena, whose face is marred by dust and sweat and blood, who strives valiantly, who errs and comes short again and again because there is no effort without error and shortcomings, who knows the great enthusiasm, the great devotions, and spends himself in a worthy cause, who at the best knows in the end the triumph of high achievement, and who at worst, if he fails, at least fails while daring greatly, knowing his place shall never be with those timid and cold souls who know neither victory or defeat."

—Theodore Roosevelt

During the administration of John Quincy Adams (1825–1829), Congress came within three votes of terminating the U.S. Patent Office. The reason: there were representatives who believed that all the good ideas had already been patented, and they wanted to save the taxpayers' money. Since then, of course, we've had technological inventions such as radios, automobiles, airplanes, televisions, copying machines, fax machines, computers, orbiting satellites, and literally millions of other new products.

If Congress could have considered closing the patent office, it shouldn't come as a surprise to anyone when people close their minds to a new idea. Knowing this, I never allowed myself to be discouraged when I was confronted with doomsayers and critics who said UCC would never get off the ground.

## Don't Keep It a Secret

Once I made up my mind to start UCC, I wasn't shy about telling my idea to others. Yet there are some people who are very secretive about starting a new business. I believe they remain close-mouthed about their future plans out of a fear of failure. They're afraid to talk about what they're going to do because if their new venture never gets off the ground, they'll lose face.

I take the opposite approach. I announced my intentions to form a national buyers' club to everyone—family, friends, and strangers. By letting the word out, I had no choice but to do what I said I was going to do. If not, *I'd lose face.*

In the writing of this book, I did the same thing. Once my decision was made to write it, I announced it at the UCC January 1990 franchise owners' meeting. By doing so, I made sure that every person in the entire organization would know about it within a matter of days. Likewise, I told my family, friends, and business associates. Now I *had* to write it! If not, I would lose face with the people in this world who are the most important to me. So now it becomes a matter of pride to finish anything that I start.

Yes, there's a slight risk that somebody might steal your idea if you prematurely announce it. This risk, however, is so slight that it's one I feel is worth taking. Frankly, the chance of someone stealing my plans to establish a buyers' club was virtually nonexistent. I could hardly get anyone to *listen* to my idea, let alone copy it!

## The Value of Free Advice

The world is full of people who always feel compelled to give advice to others. They volunteer it whether you ask for it or not. While they think they're acting out of benevolence, don't you be misled. No matter how well intentioned they may be, their advice is usually destructive. Rarely do they have the expertise to voice a meaningful opinion. So always consider the source. Ask yourself such questions as: "On what facts does he base his advice?" "What are her credentials that give her a background in this area?" "I've put a lot of thought into my plans—has this person also thought through the pertinent details?"

There are exceptions, but usually the value of free advice approximates what you pay for it (nothing).

# —3—

# GROWING PAINS

IF I HAD A WORST ENEMY, I'd encourage him to start a buyers' club from scratch. I'd tell him to mortgage his house and borrow everything he could. It would be sweet revenge, because the likelihood would be very great that he'd be wiped out. At first blush, running UCC looks like a piece of cake, but as I soon discovered, there are headaches galore.

The problem was that, in the beginning, I was getting it from both sides. The manufacturers didn't want to sell to me because they anticipated repercussions from their retail accounts, and consumers resisted becoming members because they didn't understand how we could offer merchandise to them at cost and make any money. Much of the opposition was a result of our concept being so foreign to what people were used to. They'd say, "What's the gimmick?"

"There isn't a gimmick," I'd reply. "My profit will come from the dues people pay to belong to the club."

"You mean you want me to pay dues for the privilege of buying from you?"

The more questions I was asked, and the more I tried to explain the concept, the more doubt and suspicion would

37

arise. But trial and error is an effective teacher. Over the years our original sales presentation went through a series of changes until it evolved into its present-day form. Today it takes about one hour to explain UCC and how members benefit from it. It's a formal presentation that condenses more than two hundred years of American marketing history into a sixty-minute lesson.

I discovered that it's not enough to build a better mouse-trap—somebody still has to convince the consumer. The idea to begin UCC was, by itself, a single, small step. An effective marketing system was necessary to make it a reality. We didn't simply open a club in a convenient location and sit back waiting for customers to come marching in to sign up.

We were handicapped, however, because we couldn't advertise. If we advertised the value of a UCC membership and how the club worked, local retailers would present strong opposition, and suppliers would be alienated or scared away.

Bit by bit, we built a sales organization that for some years groped around in the dark. Always pioneering, we had no path we could follow. We had to recruit, train, and develop a sales force that, in turn, would sell memberships and recruit, train, and develop still others to operate future clubs. It was a long and tedious process. As the company founder, I had no mentor to advise and encourage me. Repeatedly I would head down one avenue only to find a dead end.

The most painful part was hearing so many negative comments about UCC, when all the while I knew that what we had to offer was so good. In particular, there were accusations that we were a fly-by-night company. People felt we wouldn't be able to deliver what we promised. It wasn't fair, and it was hurtful.

As I look back, my company went through a period of severe growing pains. In hindsight, I was so involved in the day-to-day problems of our business, I wasn't aware that that's what was happening. Now I realize that every start-up business goes through a similar stage during its early years. I'm sure outsiders who look at today's UCC don't even suspect that we struggled during this difficult period of uncertainty. They see us now as a thriving enterprise—but by no means were we an overnight success. While the information contained in this chapter is specifically about my growing pains, the symptoms I will describe to you on the following pages are likely to happen to every expanding entrepreneurship. So read on, because what I experienced, you probably will too.

## What Should UCC Sell?

At first, nothing was easy. I even had difficulty trying to decide what our product line should be. Because we could sell almost anything, we had to carefully think about what we could sell best. In a normal business, say, an appliance store, a sporting goods store, or a clothing store, what to sell is a given. You sell television sets and refrigerators, golf clubs and tennis rackets, and suits and shirts. I do believe, however, that it's essential for a start-up business to give serious thought as to what market it will cater to. Should you go after the carriage trade, for example, or sell lower-end, more popularly priced merchandise? After all, when you're small, you can't have something for everybody—you're better off specializing than attempting to be a large department store.

In our infancy, we didn't want to offer a mishmash of merchandise—a dining room set here, a set of golf clubs there, a toaster oven, and so on. The decision was finally made to concentrate on selling furniture. First, it is something everybody needs. Second, furniture is a big-ticket item. Third, when a couple furnishes a home, the costs run into the thousands of dollars. And fourth, with the big markup on furniture, members could save large sums of money (more than the membership fee) with a single UCC purchase. Our initial game plan was to line up enough furniture manufacturers so we could present a selection of several lines, and sequentially do the same thing with home accessories lines. Next we would offer carpeting, drapery, home appliances, outdoor garden supplies, and other household products.

While it's true my original attraction to the Furniture Mart was that it was only an hour car trip away, my instinct to line up furniture manufacturers was a good one. Even with the wide diversification of the more than five hundred companies UCC represents today, 55 percent of our sales volume is home furnishings.

At first, the main criterion for selecting a manufacturer was based on our personal tastes for the line. During our first week at the mart, Fred and I didn't know a thing about the furniture industry. If I liked a sofa displayed in a showroom, we'd stop in and look at the line, and if he liked a bedroom set, we'd do the same. In time, we learned from our mistakes and discovered that there were several other considerations such as brand recognition, reliable delivery, proper pricing structure, service, warranties, and what kind of sales literature the company provides. My son Jack, who is now our vice president of purchasing, insists that companies supply us with attractive catalogs and, in particular, catalogs that are user-friendly but still contain the very same product information and price structure offered to retail stores. In the early days, we weren't in a position to be selective and had to take what we could get.

As our membership base began to expand and mature, it was apparent that we needed to offer a broader range of products. After all, there were only so many bedroom sets and appliances a member could buy. Much of the new merchandise that was added to our product line resulted from requests made by members. "Why doesn't UCC sell garden tractors?" one would ask. "I could use a desk for my office," another would comment.

Some products that we have tried to sell simply didn't work in our operation. Anything that's perishable won't work, so food and plants had to be ruled out. We also stay away from most clothing items, because size presents a problem. Then, too, what might be appealing in a catalog might not look good on the buyer. In addition, clothes are too seasonal, and styles change quickly. We also avoid offering products that require an exorbitant amount of paperwork, because the cost of processing an order then becomes prohibitive and would require higher membership fees. The sale of insurance policies falls into this category. What's more, our people would have to be licensed to sell them. Boats were another consideration, but we couldn't provide the assembly and service needed after the purchase, so they, too, don't work. The same is true with certain brands of lawn mowers, computers, and other mechanical products—we avoid selling anything that can't be serviced in the areas where UCC clubs exist. So while we are always aggressively looking for new companies to represent, there are restrictions that eliminate certain products.

Early on, we also made the important decision to sell quality merchandise. We quickly realized that there were far fewer things to go wrong with well-made products sold by highly reputable firms, and handling a superior product limits customer complaints. In addition, we discovered that members who had budgeted $1,000 for a sofa would often purchase a $2,000 sofa from us for that same $1,000 rather than spend $500 for their original choice. This meant that the consumers were able to own something twice as good for their $1,000. Not only would the more expensive sofa often provide more enjoyment, but due to its better quality, it was also more durable and lasted longer. The same was true with golf clubs, stereo systems, mattresses—virtually every product across the board.

## Learning the Lingo

Every industry has a language of its own. It's as if insiders want to confuse everybody else or, perhaps, make their work seem more mysterious. Physicians use Latin to make sure you don't understand. The lawyers like Latin terms too, plus many more terms that buffalo the layperson. I recently learned of a six-hundred-page dictionary with more than six thousand terms pertaining to the securities field! In recent years, a whole new language has sprung up in the computer field; fifteen years or so ago, who ever heard of bits and bytes? Every industry has its technical jargon, and the wholesale and retail industries are no different. So I suppose I should have known better when I first began meeting with manufacturers. Had I done my homework, I could have avoided some embarrassment.

I recall one such incident at the Furniture Mart when Fred and I were trying to convince a manufacturer to give us enough catalogs so each of our ten clubs could have one in its showroom. "We need one for every club," I said.

"They run us about $60 a whack," the man said. In 1972 that was a lot of money.

"I understand," I said, "and we'll pay for them."

"I'll tell you what I'll do," he told me. "I will just memo bill it, OK?"

Fred and I looked at each other, and I said, "Good idea. Memo bill it."

When we left, I asked Fred, "Do you know what he meant by a memo bill?"

"No. I was hoping you would, Jim."

Later that day, we bumped into a friend and asked him. "How soon do we have to send a check in when we're memo billed?"

"You nitwits," he good-naturedly replied. "They don't bill you. As soon as you're buying and the volume reaches a certain level, they just take the charge off for you. In the meantime, you owe them the money, but you don't have to pay it."

"That's a helluva lot better than I thought it was."

Another time, I said to a furniture rep, "I'll take six sofas, six end tables, and six of this, this, and this."

"OK," he replied, "but it's not a whole carload. We will have to individual ship it unless you want to pool car."

I had no idea what "pool car" meant. I thought perhaps I'd be able to figure it out during the course of the conversation. "OK," I said. "Will I save on that?"

"Yeah, same as you always save on it," he answered.

"I know that, but can you give me an idea of what it's costing me from your place?" I continued.

"No, but it will be significant, and I will put you with some good people."

"Sure, that's great," I said, having figured out that I'd be sharing the car in some way.

When we left, I asked somebody, "What does it mean when you 'pool car'?" (I quickly learned that the term is used to describe the transportation of two or more firms' merchandise via a single truck or railway car.)

It didn't take long before we learned the vernacular, but originally we just tried to fake it. It was hard enough convincing any manufacturer to let us sell its line, and had the furniture reps thought we were completely naive, it would have been an even more difficult task. Looking back, we probably didn't fool as many people as we thought.

## A Shopping Spree Through the Furniture Mart in a Wheelchair

I've been blessed with good health with one exception. During early 1972, I had a health problem that Preparation H no longer solved. Consequently, I spent most of my waking hours standing up, and when I did sit, I sat on a rubber doughnut. Unfortunately, nobody gets a choice about when an illness is to occur. And with the company only a few months old, it couldn't have come at a worse time. Beginning in January, I was under constant treatment. It was very debilitating, and my weight dropped from 150 pounds to 118. I was scheduled to enter the hospital in May to undergo surgery, which was purposely delayed until after the mart's showing in April.

By then, I was so weak I could barely stand for ten minutes without falling over, but I felt it was essential to be at the mart. Although everyone tried to talk me out of it, I felt it demonstrated my dedication to my franchisees, and I wasn't about to let them down. I believed they expected this much of me. Naturally, I would have preferred the comfort of my bedroom, but commitment transcended my discomfort.

During the course of a full day at the mart, one can literally walk ten miles. The only way I could do it was in a wheelchair, so Fred and my wife, Claire, took turns pushing. Although it was never my intention, the wheelchair turned out to be a terrific sales tool. People were more courteous, and there was the sympathy factor. After all, it's hard to throw a guy in a wheelchair out of a showroom.

At one manufacturer's showroom, I gave a full presentation about UCC. It wore me out, and as I was not used to sitting for so many hours at a time, my legs were cramped. I removed the shawl covering my legs, and it took a laborious effort to stand in order to stretch and take a few tentative steps. I was very weak, and my face was ashen. Two women were carefully observing me in awe. "Oh, my God," a woman said, "he can walk!"

"It's a miracle," the other said.

I winked at the manufacturer's rep and threw my weak arms in the air. "It's just as you promised," I declared. "I bought your furniture, and now I can walk again!" With that, a wave of laughter swept across the showroom.

## Selling the First Franchise on a Napkin

Right off the bat, my game plan was to set up UCC clubs all over the country. Without the capital to finance them, I decided to establish franchises. I like the franchising concept because the person running the club has a proprietary interest. I believe that very early in the game, every entrepreneur who aspires to have a national concern should begin to think about how his or her distribution system will be structured. While I knew as a franchisor I'd have less control, I also believed I'd attract better-quality people—those with an ambition to be their own boss—and the type who set no limits on their earning potential.

My first *attempt* to sell a franchise was made to Fred Wittlinger and Jack Allen, and they made a commitment to come aboard in early 1972. But this was not my first franchise sale. I don't consider a sale made until a payment of the franchise fee accompanies a signed contract. The individual who actually became the first UCC franchisee was a man from Anderson, Indiana, a city with a population of approximately fifty thousand about forty miles northeast of Indianapolis. My original conversation with him was simply to let him know what I was doing. I made no attempt to sell him.

His reaction was, "It sounds interesting. I have to find something, too, because I'm in the process of phasing out my business."

We had subsequent telephone conversations, and I finally made the suggestion that he consider a franchise with me.

"You know, I've been thinking about that, Jim," he said. "How much is it going to cost me?"

I didn't really have an exact price in mind, but I told him it would cost $10,000. There was a silence. I quickly added, "I want $5,000 down and the balance in monthly installments from your future earnings."

"OK, I'm in."

"Fine," I answered matter-of-factly, trying to conceal my jubilation. The thought that it was so easy raced through my mind. Then the salesman in me spoke out: "Come on in tomorrow morning, and I'll meet you for coffee at the Holiday Inn at nine o'clock. And be sure to bring a certified check made payable to me for $5,000."

He showed up on time, and we ordered coffee. After answering a few questions, I started to jot down a few of the details on a napkin. "Now here's how I envision our logo," I said, and drew it for him.

About a half hour into the meeting, I shook his hand: "Congratulations, Pal, you're the first in, and because you are, I'm charging you a lower franchise fee than what I'll be asking others to pay. Now I'll need your certified check."

"I didn't bring one," he apologized.

I was stunned. "What! I told you to bring a certified check. There wasn't any point in driving two hours without one."

"But with the one-hour drive and the one-hour difference in time zones, the bank wasn't open this morning when I left Anderson. I didn't want to be late . . ."

I was angry and didn't hide it. "You are not going to get the first franchise because you aren't financially capable of handling it."

"I'm sorry that I didn't bring the check, but I did bring

$5,000 in cash," he said and placed an envelope with $100 bills on the table.

I cleared my throat.

"Cash is acceptable," I answered, picking up the envelope and placing it in my briefcase. Naturally I was willing to accept cash, knowing perfectly well that cash never bounces. "But in the future, if we're going to be in business together, never pay anything by cash. It's important to pay by check so there's a paper record of the transaction. Now I congratulate you . . ."

He asked me a few more questions, and I answered them to the best of my ability. I leveled with him and said that I only had a brief sketch of what the business would really be like, and that I'd have to make it up as we went along. "I'm not sure what manufacturers we'll actually sign up," I said, "and at this time, I can't even give you a final profile of what our company will be, but we're going to give it our best, and guys like us don't fail. We'll make some mistakes, but we will succeed."

I used the money from the sale to incorporate the company, and we were off and running.

That second week in January, between the time the first franchisee came aboard and when the club was officially under way, I had visited the mart with Fred. We lined up thirty suppliers, so with a franchise in Anderson, the time had come to sign up members.

Although I advised the Anderson franchisee to lease about 2,000 square feet in a local shopping center, he rented an 1,800-square-foot, two-story brick house in a lower-middle-class area that was a mixture of commercial and residential properties. The office was in the basement, and the rest of the house contained sample furniture (the bedroom had a bedroom set, the dining room had a dining room set, etc.). Tables and chairs were put in the basement where members could read suppliers' catalogs and transact purchase orders. To keep expenses down, chairs were rented from a local funeral home—the chairs were comfortable enough, but the name of the funeral home was emblazoned on the backs! This definitely was not the image I wanted to project. Photographs were cut out of the larger catalogs that contained the most attractive color pictures and pasted on the walls.

A handful of salespeople were hired in Anderson, and by January 15 they were pounding the pavement and making telephone calls to set up evening appointments for sales presentations. During the first thirty days in operation, twenty-six memberships were sold. Of these, four canceled. They probably got buyer's remorse—either that, or they visited the showroom and saw those funeral home chairs. We probably would have lost others too, had more stopped in and seen the chairs.

To sell other franchises, I used Anderson as an example of what could be done operating out of an old house with rented furniture. Before that franchise had been in business for a full month, a contract was signed with Fred Wittlinger and Jack Allen, giving them the exclusive rights for Valparaiso. The price was $12,500, and they gave me $5,000 as a down payment. During the first year, Fred kept his job with IBM, and Jack practiced law and served as a city judge. They bought a small building, put up paneling, ceilings, and shelving, and did a lot of painting. Jane Wittlinger and Jody Allen did the bookkeeping and operated the showroom; Fred and Jack worked on Saturdays and weeknights.

The third franchise went for $15,000 in Joliet, Illinois. By the end of the first year, I had sold eleven, mainly in small towns and cities in Indiana, Illinois, and Ohio. I did not anticipate so many would be sold during the first year. I was proud of what we had accomplished, yet when I looked at the map of the United States with flags representing UCC franchises, I was very much aware that we had simply scratched the surface.

## Establishing a Sales Organization

Without being able to advertise what UCC did, I couldn't expect that simply hanging up a shingle would be enough to attract hordes of eager consumers wanting to be members. So

I figured that if the consumer didn't come to UCC, we'd go to the consumer. It was this thinking that led me to set up a direct-sales organization that would call on prospects at their homes to sell memberships. As I mentioned earlier, nothing happens until something is sold.

Even though we had a wonderful product, at first it was not an easy thing to sell. Admittedly, much of the problem was my lack of experience in setting up a direct-sales organization. The product's uniqueness also contributed to the difficulty because the consumer had no basis on which to compare its value. While most salespeople voice complaints about having too much competition, we were perhaps handicapped by the *lack of competition*. Nobody was familiar with being a member of a club to which dues were paid for the right to buy merchandise. Imagine how difficult it would be, for example, to sell life insurance if no one knew what it was. That's what we were up against. We had to spend a disproportionate amount of our time educating prospects about wholesaling and retailing in America in order to lead into what we were selling.

There were several reasons for making the decision to sell in the home. First, we believed that buying a membership was a family buying decision. Back then, while the man made the money, the woman did the shopping—thus it was a joint decision. Second, the vast majority of our product line was home furnishings, so again a joint decision was expected. Plus, in the home, our trained salespeople could determine a prospect's needs for furniture as well as the prospect's taste level. Part of the presentation included asking what the prospect planned to buy in the future. Sitting at the kitchen table or in the den, the salesperson would flip through his or her presentation manual, all the while making comments such as, "It looks as though you'll be in the market for a dishwasher," and, "Now that your children are older, you'll want to consider replacing your den furniture." By observing a couple's lifestyle, it was easy to get a feel for their unique needs.

UCC was no different from other direct-sales organizations in that we, too, faced the common problem of getting our foot in the door. Our salespeople tried everything from sending out mailers to cold-calling prospects on the telephone to set up appointments. From the start, our salespeople were trained to understand the ratios and to work them. It was ingrained in their minds that making so many calls and setting up so many appointments would result in a certain number of sales. For instance, if $x$ amount of brochures are mailed out, $y$ amount of people will respond by calling us. Or $x$ amount of telephone interviews will generate $y$ amount of sales presentations. Of these presentations, 50 percent will become members. Knowing this, a salesperson could determine how many brochures or phone interviews it took to make one sale. With this information, a salesperson could determine what his or her time was worth on an hourly basis.

This is nothing new. All professional salespeople understand how the numbers work in their field. Once known, earnings can be projected by the number of hours worked. In the long run, the numbers are very reliable.

There were two main hurdles to selling memberships in the home. First, people usually prefer to occupy their evenings in ways other than listening to a salesperson. In fact, most people prefer to avoid outside salespeople altogether. This meant that a UCC salesperson frequently would arrive for an evening appointment only to find that nobody was home. Or if somebody was, no lights were on, and prospects were observed hiding behind curtains. No-shows are not only discouraging, they rob a salesperson of his or her most precious commodity—prime selling time.

Second, most people are suspicious when a salesperson knocks on their door. In all probability, they fear the unscrupulous peddler who misrepresents products to make sales. In truth, the vast majority of American salespeople are honest individuals; the stereotype of the fast-talking canvasser stems from the turn-of-the-century snake oil pitchmen. As a consequence, the general distrust of door-to-door salespeople prevails to this day. People worry about what recourse there is if they buy something that isn't what it was cracked up to be. For good reason, the term *fly-by-night* vividly conjures a seller who is here today and gone tomorrow. In our case, a doubting Thomas might wonder if the UCC showroom really does exist, and if so, whether it really does have "bargain-filled catalogs." It is no wonder that many of our in-home sales presentations resulted in cases of buyer's remorse, a change of mind by the customer after having made a buying decision.

From a company's viewpoint, it is difficult to control an outside sales force. It was only a matter of time before I found out firsthand how a lack of control can create headaches. Our biggest problem was when an interested party inquired about a specific manufacturer's line. Knowing that a "yes" would generate a positive response, some of our salespeople said whatever was necessary to sufficiently whet the prospect's appetite and close the sale. This is gross misrepresentation, and it always came back to haunt us.

The most flagrant incident I can recall happened in one of our clubs. During a conversation after the prospect had signed a membership form and written out his check, the subject of fishing was brought up. The prospect asked if it would be possible to purchase fingerling bass from UCC to stock his ten-acre pond. The salesperson assured him that the club could accommodate him. Sure enough, two months later the prospect came into the club to buy his fish. It was quite embarrassing for the club owner to have to explain that UCC did not sell fish to stock ponds.

There was no way to police everything that was said in the field, and we could only respond to problems after the fact. Even though our policy was to give full refunds to dissatisfied members, in most cases the damage was already done. Naturally, we fired the offending salesperson, which cut down on repeat performances. But in the meantime, we also had to deal with the problem of determining who was telling the truth. Did the salesperson really say what the prospect accused him of saying? Did the prospect only hear what he wanted to hear? Only when we'd observed a pattern could we positively know who was guilty as accused.

We were, however, able to police some unscrupulous behavior. One time, for instance, we were able to make a special purchase of sewing machines made by the Morse Electrofonic Sewing Machine Co. The retail price of the machines was $495 as advertised in several family magazines, including a half page in *Reader's Digest*. The company's dealers would sell a sewing machine for $200 to $300 and still make money on it because the wholesale price was only $90. I was astounded that the markup was so high, and I purchased a carload of them to display and inventory at our clubs. We'd show the sewing machine and the advertisements to our members and say, "What do you think the real cost is? $300? $250? $200?" They would guess as low as $200. And we'd say, "No, it's $90. That's what you can buy it for at UCC." This was an excellent way for us to reemphasize the value of being a member, and the sewing machines became a big sales item for us.

One of our franchisees put the sewing machine in his front window, with the advertisement stating the $495 price tag, and a big sign also stated it was marked down to $90. When people came in off the street to purchase it, he'd say, "Oh, I'm sorry, but only members can buy it for that price." This generated a response: "A member? Member of what?"—his opening to sell a membership. On a visit to his club, I saw the sign and said UCC does not permit bait-and-switch tactics and to stop doing it at once. So some things could be controlled, but what was said in the home could not.

## An Innovative Marketing Approach

For six years, UCC memberships were sold in the home. During this period, our companywide closing ratio was 50 percent, a respectable figure for any sales organization. This number, however, does not reflect the high cancellation rate and recurring headaches we suffered. Still, the business was growing, and we continued to sign up more and more suppliers.

Like any new business, we had our ups and downs, yet we kept plugging away, always trying to devise ways to improve our selling and servicing. Our source for new ideas was mainly the clubs themselves. Members would make suggestions about what kinds of products we should carry, franchisees and salespeople would come up with better ways to sell, and so on. We operated like a family business, with a lot of caring and sharing. When one club came up with something that worked well, it was brought to our attention at the home office, and if it had merit, it would eventually be used by all franchises.

There were exceptions. One such person who did not care to share was the franchisee in Albany, New York. When his sales suddenly skyrocketed, we called him to inquire about his remarkable production. Reluctantly, he admitted that his sales force was no longer making in-home sales presentations. Instead, prospects were invited to the club to tour the facilities, observe sample products that were on display, and glance through price catalogs. At that time, we had an unwritten rule that nonmembers were not permitted to visit a club's showroom; however, I said that I wanted to know more about what he was doing, because if it worked so well for him, it might be something to be used by every franchise. He agreed—on the condition that for the use of his system, a fee of $25 for every membership sale would be paid to him. I was furious, and I let him know it.

I repeatedly stressed to him that one of our great strengths was that new ideas were always shared throughout the organization, making other clubs and UCC stronger, so that everyone benefited. He still refused to share.

John Spath, an ex-policeman who operates our Youngstown, Ohio, club, called the Albany franchise and asked if he could visit for a few days to observe what is now referred to as the "tour." He was flatly turned down. John, however, was persistent and sent two of his salespeople, who, posing as prospects, did some surveillance. Their mission was to find out exactly what a tour was. They evidently gave themselves away by calling to request a tour because in those days it was a rare occasion when anyone *called us*, and when they were given a tour, it was purposely done wrong to mislead them.

(This information was later given to us by Don Daley, who worked as a salesperson in Albany and now operates his own franchise in Westminster, Colorado.) Still later, our Beaver Falls, Pennsylvania, franchisee visited Albany, and while he also was not privy to the "real" tour, more information about it was gained.

In time we learned enough about the tour to understand that a presentation made to a group consisting of two to six couples was more effective than a corresponding number of one-to-one presentations in the prospects' homes. That same year, Don Daley became a salesperson at our Indianapolis club, and he gave us still more information about the tour. It wasn't long before a major falling out occurred with the Albany franchisee. It had more to do with two sets of books he was keeping than with his unwillingness to share the tour, and his franchise agreement was canceled.

No one person or franchise is credited for the present tour. While the first tour was made in Albany, what has evolved is much different. Soon every UCC club was using the tour, and to this day, presentations are no longer made in the home. Don Daley informed us that the original tour was a five-page presentation; it has since been expanded to thirty-seven pages. Through trial and error and feedback from all of our franchises, the tour that has evolved barely resembles the original one.

Today, a public relations director (the official title given to a UCC salesperson) makes telephone calls to prospects, and after giving a brief explanation about the company, he or she mails UCC literature to interested parties. A few days later, the director calls back and invites the prospect and his or her spouse to come as guests to have a tour of the club. A visitor's pass is mailed to be presented at the door. When the guests arrive, they are greeted by the director. The guests generally arrive at 7:30 P.M. and the tour begins at 7:45.

The franchisee or club manager makes a presentation to the group of prospects. This goes on for about one hour. The directors are not present because they are in another room making good use of their time by telephoning prospects to schedule future tours. When the presentation has ended, each individual director meets with the prospects on a one-on-one basis to answer questions and, with them, browses through the manufacturers' library, demonstrating how to look up merchandise and prices in catalogs. This is the fun part. People stare wide-eyed at the differences between the wholesale prices and retail prices. This enables people to get a feel of how the club works and, most importantly, how much can be saved when they are members. Finally, the director helps the prospects complete the membership form.

While the closing ratio is still around 50 percent, the tour presentation has eliminated many of the headaches previously experienced by selling in the homes of prospects. For starters, we now have control of what is said. No longer can anyone make a wild statement that UCC has a supplier that will stock a pond or lake with fish, because there are witnesses present. Additionally, there is tangible evidence that the club truly exists and is all it's cracked up to be. In summary, a much more professional format exists to present what we offer our members.

## The Procrastinator

People have a tendency to put off buying decisions. This is especially true when they buy something outside their area of expertise. Professionals, such as neurosurgeons or high-powered business executives who are used to making bold decisions on the job, might be hesitant to buy a life insurance policy, a computer system, a house, or an expensive diamond ring. Imagine the difficulty one who knew nothing about diamonds would have, for instance, in making a buying decision about such a gem. The buyer must determine whether its value is worth the asking price, and this puts him or her in the precarious position of having to rely on the seller's representations. It should also be noted that the ownership of a diamond is strictly a luxury—it is not a necessity. Nobody *has* to own one. The more familiar a person is with a particular product, the easier it is to make a buying decision. A corporate executive who purchases a large fleet of cars on a regular basis probably will not exhibit the slightest hesitancy whatsoever when placing a seven-digit order. Likewise, the average consumer struggles considerably more with the purchase of his first car than his tenth car!

At UCC, when each membership is sold, it is a first-of-its-kind buying decision for the client. Again, being a pioneer in our industry has its unique set of problems. When a new club is opened, the unfamiliarity is at its peak. Not only has a prospect never heard about UCC, he or she probably doesn't know anyone who has. It is only with the passing of time that things get easier. Once a club is established, there are enough members in the area that names can be given when a prospect inquires as to who already belongs. Also, satisfied members provide referrals of relatives and friends. In time, recommendations by existing members are a club's best source of new members. So, as the club plants its roots in an area and builds a solid membership base, sales resistance diminishes.

Just the same, when people don't feel a sense of urgency to buy a product or service, they're prone to want to "think things over." There is a natural tendency to delay a purchase due to the fear of making a wrong decision. By playing it safe and doing nothing, people think they can avoid making a mistake. In truth, however, procrastination can be an even bigger mistake. Depending on the product, a built-in sense of urgency prevails. For instance, when a prospect prolongs the decision to buy a life insurance policy, horrendous consequences can occur in the event of a premature death. Likewise, to delay the purchase of a listed security can result in not being able to execute a transaction at a certain price due to the fluctuation of the stock market. And in real estate, the inability to make a decision may cause a couple to lose a particular home because, during that indecision, somebody else buys it. A good salesperson realizes that it is a disservice not to point out the dangers that are likely to occur when a buying decision is delayed. Many people view such selling as high-pressure. In truth, though, it can be in the best interest of the buyer.

When people procrastinate, they generally end up not buying when perhaps they should. What happens is that the law of diminishing returns sets in. As time lapses, they fail to retain all the benefits that were presented to them. For example, immediately following a two-hour presentation by a life insurance agent that covers estate planning with the complicated tax and legal consequences, the prospect will undoubtedly have a better understanding of the product than a day later. The more time that expires after the presentation, the less information the prospect retains. Because he or she remembers fewer benefits than at the time of the presentation, it is less likely that the prospect will buy. It is far better to make a buying decision when all of the facts are fresh in one's mind. Men and women who serve in high executive positions share this opinion, and, in part, this decisiveness is a contributing factor to their success.

All successful salespeople also understand that procrastination works against them as well as their prospects. The pro knows people simply "cool off." The longer the period that lapses after the sales presentation, the less is the chance that a transaction will occur. Convincing prospects to buy now when they have expressed their intention to put off buying is a delicate situation. If, at this point, the salesperson comes on too strong, the buyers will feel pressured and back away. Or if the seller ends up closing the sale, the buyer may later feel resentful and cancel the order. There's a lot of truth in the saying "A man convinced against his will is of the same opinion still."

I believe a salesperson must handle sales of this nature with the utmost finesse—a thin line exists between high-pressure selling and professional selling that serves the best interests of the buyer. Indecisiveness makes people feel uncomfortable—they would like to arrive at a conclusion—and it's the salesperson's job to help them get there. To close a high percentage of these borderline sales, the seller must make the buyer believe that there is something to gain by buying *today*. Certainly it takes more than saying, "You must buy now because I won't sell it to you later." There must be a logical reason for a prospect to be convinced that he or she must take decisive action.

At UCC, we are fortunate to have a built-in reason. We give a logical explanation to each person who participates in a tour about why a decision is required today. What is actually said is something that neither I nor anyone else contemplated prior to starting our business. It really happened by accident, but it's such a compelling and honest reason that it has become a permanent part of every sales presentation at all UCC clubs.

What appeared to be a disaster in Muncie, Indiana, turned out to be a wonderful lesson and truly a blessing in disguise. In 1975, after a great deal of persuasion, I was able to sign up Kimball Piano as a UCC supplier. Back then, it was one of the leading manufacturers of fine pianos, and we were very proud to sell their seven-foot baby grand piano, which had a $7,995 sticker price, for $4,200. That is a large sum of money, and although we didn't sell many of them, the line was prestigious to carry. Members liked to browse through the Kimball catalog, perhaps more curious about the cost of a fine piano than wanting to buy one.

One member in Muncie was observed writing down some information from the Kimball catalog and mentioned to the club's manager that he'd "sleep on it before making a decision." After leaving the club, the member walked down the street and into the showroom of a Kimball Piano dealer. He asked to see a particular ebony baby grand, and when he was quoted a price of $7,995, he asked, "What kind of deal can you give me if I pay cash?" The dealer quoted a price of $6,800.

"That's not good enough."

"If I sold it to you any cheaper, I couldn't make any money on the sale," the dealer replied.

"That's not true," the customer said. "You're only paying $4,200 for it." He actually quoted him the wholesale price to the exact penny.

The dealer was astounded and said, "Where did you get that figure?"

"I belong to UCC, and I saw it in the catalog."

The two men went back and forth for several minutes, and finally, in a state of frustration, the dealer declared, "If you take me to your club and prove to me that you can buy it for that amount, that's what I'll sell it to you for."

The two men went back to the club, and the dealer was introduced as the member's brother-in-law who was interested in joining the club. "Can I bring him in and show him around?"

"Yeah, sure," replied the manager. (The Muncie club was a spin-off franchise from our Anderson franchise.)

The two men promptly marched over to the Kimball catalog, and right there, in black and white, the dealer was able to see that his retail price was no competition against UCC. With that, he shouted in anger, "How dare they do this!" With that, he stormed out of the club.

"But what about the piano you're going to sell me?" the member pleaded.

The dealer shouted, "Take it and shove it."

The next morning, I received a call from the owner of Kimball Piano, who gave me a rundown of what happened in Muncie. "I can't believe what you're saying," I said, "but I can't deny it either. Would you give me the courtesy of permitting me to investigate it and get back to you within twenty-four hours?"

He consented. Before driving down to Muncie that afternoon, I called the club and asked the manager to invite the member to be present the following day. "Tell him the founder of the company wants to meet him."

My first meeting was a private session with the manager. "I want you to tell me exactly what happened. And be honest with me."

He started to give me a song and dance. "Look," I said, "no b.s. What you did affects the entire company, and we're going to have to pay for your mistake if it can't be resolved. Tell me what happened . . . from the beginning."

After hearing the entire story, I sat down with the member.

"You don't have a membership anymore. I'm revoking it. You are out!"

As an afterthought, I asked him, "By the way, did you get the piano?"

"No."

"You deserve a piano. Now you can go out and pay whatever you can. Full retail."

We gave him a refund of his membership fees, and I fired the manager.

I called Kimball and apologized: "It didn't happen exactly as you told me, but it was close enough, and, boy, do I have egg all over my face now."

"Look, Jim," he said, like a gentleman. "These things will happen."

"Yes, and I wish I could guarantee you it could never happen again, but I can't. It happened with your fine and highly recognizable product, and I am very embarrassed. I will immediately insist that every club send all Kimball literature to you at once. I am terribly sorry that we can't do business now. There may be a time in the future when we may, so I want you to remember that we respect what you are, and, hopefully, you will recognize us for what we are."

He expressed his appreciation, and that was the end of it. Interestingly, in 1989 my son Jack signed up Kimball again. Today they make a smaller, apartment-sized piano. I asked Jack if the subject was brought up that we used to represent Kimball. Jack informed me that he was unaware that we had ever represented Kimball. He also said that nothing was mentioned to him by the company.

Now, getting back to the lesson we learned. As a result of what happened with the Kimball dealer, we specifically instruct new members not to quote our wholesale prices to retailers, nor should our prices be used as a tool to bargain for a deal. Additionally, during the tour, we state that in the past, after hearing what we had to offer, some people would stop in to see a local retailer and try to get a better price on a bedroom set or whatever, using the UCC price from which to negotiate. "This is why you are asked to make a buying decision today," we tell them. "We can't afford to antagonize local retailers and have them file complaints with our suppliers. Our members abide by this rule, because this is *their* club." Guests are also told that if a decision is not made to join that day (or night), they will not be eligible to be nominated for a membership for a seven-year period.

Some people balk and say they want to think it over, discuss it with their attorney, and so on. No matter what reason they give for not wanting to make a buying decision, we inform them that this is our rule. If somebody accuses us of using high-pressure tactics, they are told, "Either I didn't explain what we do properly, or you don't understand what it is that we do. In either case, we wind up with somebody who isn't going to be a member. Now, we understand how busy you are, so please understand that we are not going to solicit you. Your name will be placed on a list, and you cannot join UCC under any circumstances for the next seven years."

It is also pointed out that UCC has an obligation to its existing membership. If guests are permitted to visit retailers and shop around to compare prices before they join, the club would lose suppliers, which, in turn, hurts its members. "If you were to join UCC, I am sure you would want this rule to be enforced," they are told.

A while ago, a close friend of mine came in for a tour and came back the next day to sign up. "You know the rules, sir," he was informed. "You aren't eligible to be a member for seven more years."

"We'll see," he said. "I'm a personal friend of Jim Gagan's."

"Our rule applies to everyone," the club franchisee told him.

"I'm sure Jim will let me join. I'll call him."

I explained to him that I had no choice but to abide by our UCC policy. If not, we'd be accused of lying to people in order to pressure them into joining. Naturally, there's a temptation for a new franchisee or a director to accept somebody who later comes back waving his or her money in the air. But the first time we make an exception, our policy goes down the drain—and so does our integrity.

## Change Is Constant

Like all new enterprises, we had our share of growing pains. We experimented, and after some trial and error, we were able to figure out what worked best for us. For instance, for the first six months of 1972, our members could buy custom-ordered furniture and only had to pay 25 percent down. This meant that a $125 deposit could purchase a $500 sofa, including one that was ordered in green with yellow stripes and orange polka dots. By the time the sofa came in, a hundred different things had happened—the couple got divorced, went bankrupt, etc.—and, as a consequence, we got stuck with the sofa. Custom-ordered furniture is a matter of personal taste, and it therefore has little resale value. After we were forced to eat many custom orders, I had to write a letter to every member and explain that we could no longer do business in this manner. I announced that a full payment must accompany all future orders. Because I was up-front with them, they willingly accepted the new rule.

I think it's important for a beginning business owner to recognize that nothing is permanently cast in stone. An organization must be flexible and be able to go with the flow. Nothing in a new business is constant—except change.

## Double-Digit Inflation

During the first half of 1972, the prime rate was around 5 percent. By mid-September it was 10 percent, marking the first time in modern times when it reached double-digit figures. It fluctuated for the rest of the decade and peaked at a record high of 21½ percent in December 1981. I was dancing in the streets. Inflation works in our favor, because it creates an acute awareness of the shrinking dollar. During a tour, prospects are asked, "Does anyone here remember when a gallon of gasoline cost thirty cents? Does anyone here have a mortgage at 6 percent or less?" Perhaps the best lesson Americans ever received on inflation was given by President Reagan on national television. He placed a dollar bill on his desk and said it was the 1970 dollar. Next to it, he put down a pile of thirty-six pennies. He explained that the 1980 dollar bill, even though it looks the same as the 1970 bill, only bought thirty-six cents worth of goods.

Unlike his predecessors, Gerald Ford and Jimmy Carter, Reagan stayed away from fancy slogans; instead he made America stand tall. First, it was Ford who came up with a cute campaign promise he called WIN—Whip Inflation Now. But he didn't whip inflation, and he wasn't reelected. Then Carter came along and campaigned on the theme that there was a general malaise in the country and "less was best." He told Americans that they must tighten their belts. Instead of two-car families, his solution was to have one car for each family. Four years later, it turned out the country *was* sick— it was sick of *Carter*, and Reagan was elected president. Reagan restored the American dream, which has always been that tomorrow will be better. By accenting the positive, he reinstilled in Americans the national pride that had disappeared during the 1970s.

Long before the government found a solution for how to deal with inflation, millions of Americans were searching for their own answers. Inflation was a cancer that was eating away at everyone's financial health, and it was a disease that could not be cured by slogans. It was part of this anger that helped launch UCC. We listened very carefully to a loud chorus across the land that cried out, "We've had enough of the government's nonsense. If you can't do it for us, it's time for us to find our own solutions." We went to these people and showed them how we could get rid of the inflation that infested their pocketbooks. We provided a smarter and better way to get more for their hard-earned dollars. Consequently, they wouldn't have to do with less after all. This is the key reason why UCC became the success it is today. We identified a need—a *true* need—and we filled it better than anyone else.

# —4—

# SOME BAD GUYS
# WEAR BADGES, TOO

"HI, I'M FROM THE GOVERNMENT, and I'm here to help you."

If you believe that line, you're probably still waiting for the check that's in the mail.

I don't have anything against the government. With all its imperfections, the system we have in the United States is undeniably the best in the world. In fact, I'm sure that there is no other place on this planet where I could have started UCC and succeeded. I love America. I've just had it with bureaucrats.

For the past twenty years, UCC has had run-ins with dozens of contemptible civil servants, who, because they didn't understand our business, have caused us much aggravation and grief. So often they seem to have forgotten that their job is to serve the general public and promote free enterprise, not hinder it. But because the UCC concept is so unusual, they have attacked us as if under orders to take no prisoners.

Much of the flak we get from city, county, and state governments is a result of complaints lodged by local retailers who feel threatened by our presence. Often the problem arises when a merchant who owns or manages a store hears about the opening of a local club and is dead set against having us as a competitor. Until a UCC club is established, it's viewed with apprehension—we're the outsider who comes to town, and we're expected to cause havoc with the status quo.

Then, too, every so often there's a member who signs up during the tour and later isn't sure whether he or she made the right decision. After all, who doesn't question a buying decision now and then? A few weeks later, this doubting Thomas places his first order to test us, and lo and behold, something goes wrong. A supplier goofs up, and the order is delayed; the merchandise has been discontinued; something gets damaged en route to the club; and so on. Unfortunately, when it's a member's first order, and although we haven't done anything wrong, with this particular individual our credibility may be lost.

While the vast majority of our members are true believers, when such a problem occurs, we may end up with a member who thinks we're a big rip-off and wants nothing more to do with us. He or she might even go so far as to file a complaint with the attorney general's office. If it's a new club and several complaints of this nature come in, it creates a lot of suspicion about UCC. Our policy is to resolve all problems that our members have. We don't want anybody to be unhappy. It's our policy to do what's right for every member. However, when complaints are registered with a particular government agency that's unfamiliar with who we are, we're made out to be the bad guys. Of course, complaints are also filed against the most reputable, bluest of blue-chip companies. Unfortunately, with a new company, a hanging party quickly forms, even though we live in a land where a person is supposed to be innocent until proven guilty. No bureaucrat has the right to coerce and intimidate an American citizen.

I understand why retailers feel threatened, and I don't expect them to put out the welcome mat for us. However, in a free-enterprise society, the law of supply and demand is what dictates who gets into the marketplace—and, above all, *who succeeds in the marketplace*. In America, having a competitive edge is not a sufficient reason to attempt to curtail a newcomer from entering the marketplace. On the contrary, this is what makes our system work. If not, there would be only one automobile company, one insurance company, one newspaper, one grocery chain, and so on.

When a UCC club opens, we're the new kid on the block, and like any other new enterprise, we suffer from a lack of recognition that well-recognized businesses have going for them. Sometimes unjust rumors and complaints can cause overzealous bureaucrats to shoot first and then ask questions. There are times when they have to be reminded that their job as civil servants is to act in the best interests of *all the people*.

During UCC's early days, I've had several eyeball-to-eyeball encounters with bureaucrats who were quick to make accusations and threats to put me out of business. They did so before even having the slightest inkling about what UCC was. It's a horrendous injustice to a struggling entrepreneur to be subjected to harassment of this nature and, in particular, to be slapped with a cease-and-desist order that, if executed, could wreck his or her life. I sometimes wonder if the powers that be understand the ramifications of their rash behavior. After all, when innocent businesspeople are hit with a bum rap that closes their doors, their reputation is ruined, their employees lose their jobs, and their entire family suffers. When this happens to a person who knows he or she has not done anything wrong, it's an agonizing experience.

When a businessperson is mistreated and unjustly threatened with a cease-and-desist order by a government agency, I don't believe he or she should simply roll over and play dead. I advocate that people stand up for their rights. If I made an innocent mistake, tell me. Give me an opportunity to correct what I have done wrong. After all, America is a democracy and a land of opportunity for all.

## The Lion and the Lamb

"The lion and the lamb may lie down together, but the lamb won't get much sleep."

One of my favorite celebrities, Woody Allen, gets the credit for that delightful quote. It's a dandy, and so descriptive of the nervous feeling many businesspeople experience when dealing with bureaucrats.

Depending upon the nature of your business, there are certain government employees who have the power to put you out of business. With this in mind, you must learn to work either with them or around them. What you can never do is ignore them. They are a permanent fixture in the real world of business, and while it is likely that you will never feel altogether comfortable with them, they're not about to go away.

Of course, every businessperson must abide by the rules of the Internal Revenue Service. I have no complaints in this department (although I don't always agree on how our tax dollars are spent). The federal government establishes a tax code, and whether anybody thinks it's fair or not, it's the law for everyone. Yet, depending on the nature of one's business, a *change* in the tax code can have a devastating effect. Witness, for example, how recent revisions regarding tax shelters affected the investment community. But that's the way it is with the IRS. A businessperson must learn to make necessary adjustments as revisions pertain to his or her business. The collection of income taxes is essential to the welfare of our country, so I choose not to make any further comments about the IRS.

In many industries, such as the selling of insurance, real estate, securities, drugs, food, and liquor, the participants are required to be licensed. Similarly, so are professionals such as accountants, doctors, and lawyers. The reasons for such regulation are obvious, and I have no qualms about them. But what I do object to are the overly ambitious bureaucrats who have flagrantly intimidated conscientious, law-abiding citizens who were not in violation of the law, but were only suspected of wrongdoing or were simply misunderstood.

A real estate broker once told me about how the riot act was read to her when an irate home owner filed a complaint with the local real estate board. "Before I could even voice my side of the story," the broker said, "I was informed that my license was in grave jeopardy of being revoked." As the mother of three children, the middle-aged widow was terrified that she could lose her right to engage in her livelihood. This is a threat that one does not take lightly. "My hot-headed client's home had been on the market for eight months," she lamented, "and when an offer by an unqualified buyer failed to materialize, the blame was placed squarely on me. The seller made ridiculous accusations that I inappropriately wrote up the contract, which, in turn, caused the deal to fall through. While I was eventually able to prove my innocence, over the course of a month I was on the verge of a nervous breakdown. This incident occurred six years ago, and to this day I quiver in the presence of somebody from the real estate board."

The chairman of the board of a multibillion-dollar life insurance company headquartered in Chicago told me about a similar tongue-lashing he received during a telephone conversation with an Ohio Department of Insurance investigator: "A resident of Ohio accused one of our Michigan agents of crossing the state border and soliciting business without a license. Naturally, we don't condone such behavior, but with several thousand agents across the country, we can't police what each of them does in the field.

" 'The department won't tolerate activity of this nature,' the investigator shouted at me over the telephone.

" 'I can assure you we don't either,' " I replied.

" 'I want you in my office tomorrow morning at ten o'clock sharp, and we'll discuss the matter in person.'

" 'Tomorrow at ten,' I explained, 'I'm scheduled for two early-morning meetings . . .'

" 'Cancel them,' the investigator snapped.

" 'I have people coming in from out of town, and I'm not sure they can be contacted on such short notice.'

" 'That's up to you,' he challenged. 'However, if you're not in my office at exactly ten o'clock sharp, ten, I'm going to pull your company's license. Do I make myself perfectly clear?'

" 'But . . .'

" 'You heard me, mister. I'll put your company out of business in Ohio. Understand?'

" 'Yessir.'

"Needless to say, I had to rearrange a hectic schedule, but I was on the company plane to Columbus early the next morning. As I suspected, the complaint turned out to be nothing more than a misunderstanding, and we solved it in only a matter of minutes. Nonetheless, I had no choice but to abide by the SOB's request. Ohio is too big a market for us to write off because some hotshot bureaucrat gets his kicks by throwing his weight around."

Another friend of mine owns a fine restaurant in Chicago's Loop area. While his kitchen is always spic-and-span, he gets paranoid whenever somebody from the health department comes around to do a routine inspection. "In the old days," he explained, "the inspectors always had their palms extended, and if a restaurateur didn't take care of them, he'd fail the inspection. Although we've come a long way since those days, they still make me nervous because they have the authority to put me out of business—and *they know it*. They act as if they know more about the restaurant business than I do, and they resent the fact that I make so much more money than they do. Consequently, they thrive on being in a position to make my life miserable. What they fail to take into account is the long hours I work and the amount of investment I have in this place."

There are those times when it's necessary to tolerate the company of arrogant bureaucrats because you must deal with them on a regular basis. When so, be prepared to be on the receiving end of a lot of grief; sometimes you have little choice but to take it. Just recognize it as one of life's annoyances that each of us must endure from time to time. There are other occasions, however, when you can and *must* fight back, no matter how much of a licking you'll take defending yourself.

## Never Attack the Lion Unless You Intend to Slay Him

When facing a showdown with a bureaucrat I make no threats I do not intend to execute. I'm not one to bluff, the only exception being during an occasional game of poker, which, keep in mind, is only a game. But when the stakes are high, as they are in a confrontation with a powerful bureaucracy that can put you under, it is unwise to purposely invoke fury— unless you are dead certain that you are 100 percent right. Your best weapon is the absolute knowledge that you have dotted every *i* and crossed every *t* so carefully that you cannot lose. Only when dealing from such awesome strength should you wear your armor and lodge a full-scale war.

Over the years, I've met head-on with bureaucrats who were possessed with a single objective—to terminate UCC. They had no right to act with such vindictiveness, and I refused to tolerate it. Of course, on such occasions, I always had one thing going for me. I knew without a shadow of a doubt that I had not done anything wrong. If I or somebody in the company had been guilty, it would have been an entirely different story. I'd be the first one to admit it, and I would instantly make whatever change was necessary to be in the right. But what I won't put up with is having somebody out to crucify me when I am innocent. And when I'm right, I will give the opposition the fight of his or her life. On matters of this nature, I see no gray areas. I am either right or I am wrong. When I'm right, whoever attacks me had better be prepared to withstand a counterattack that, I promise, will be more fierce than the one launched against me.

My first battle with bureaucrats of major consequence occurred about ten months after UCC had opened in 1972, when I received a cease-and-desist order in the mail from the Indiana Commissioner of Securities. The order stated that United Consumers Club had violated a certain statute of the state's securities commission code pertaining to the issuance and sale of unregistered securities. When I finished reading the letter, my hands began to tremble, my face flushed, and I felt a tight knot in my stomach. Thinking that I had misunderstood it, I read it a second time. And then I became angry. Still shaking, I called my attorney, Byron Chudom, and read the letter to him. He shared my conviction that UCC did not sell securities.

"Is there any chance that we could have done something wrong and unknowingly violated a state securities regulation?" I asked.

"Let me research it," Byron replied.

A hearing date was set in Indianapolis for the following week, so we had time to do our homework.

The next day, Byron reported, "We know that UCC doesn't sell anything remotely resembling securities, but we have to convince them that we don't."

"What if we can't?" I asked, wanting to know our downside.

"Their authority is absolute," he answered.

Byron explained that the securities division's position was to classify anyone who purchased a membership as having made an investment in UCC. A few years previously, a similar case had been made against the Green Stamp Co., a company that gave a premium in the form of stamps to customers who made purchases at retail stores. In the Green Stamp case, it was argued that consumers were, in effect, buying a security because the transaction represented a promise to be delivered by the company at a future date.

"It's absurd to make such a comparison to UCC," I exclaimed. "We no more sell an investment in our firm than the Chicago Cubs do when a season-ticket holder purchases tickets for summer and autumn games. And what about owning an American Express card? It's a one- or two-year membership that, for a fee, entitles a cardholder to realize a service to be performed in the future. They may as well classify American Express as a security, too."

The hearing was scheduled for one-thirty and during our two-hour drive to the state capital, there was plenty of time for Byron to update me on his research. I was positive that we had not done anything wrong, and I was infuriated that it was costing me so much time and money to prove our innocence.

We arrived twenty minutes early for the hearing but waited until after two o'clock before we were called to appear before the commissioner, a somewhat pompous man who had been appointed by the governor to head the securities department. He was flanked by two young attorneys, who appeared to be chomping at the bit, both eager to draw blood—mine. One of them read the cease-and-desist order and inquired whether we had any questions about it.

My attorney stated that we had researched their interpretation of the law, and he explained that what we sold was indeed not a security. He pointed out how it was plainly evident that UCC had been mislabeled. In an attempt to illustrate that our service was a nonsecurity, Byron then proceeded to go into a lengthy explanation about what we were. I was unable to remain silent, and I interrupted him to interject my comments, too. As I previously mentioned, giving an explanation is not nearly as effective as a presentation and, in particular, when the explanation is in only a capsule form. However, considering that my audience was hostile, I was in no mood to make an actual sales presentation.

I even made my analogies about baseball season tickets and American Express cards, but the commissioner and his two assistants remained unconvinced. I could sense that, no matter what I said, as far as they were concerned it was a closed issue. Such a speculation made me fume, and the more I talked, the angrier I became. It was past three-thirty, and I continued to talk.

Finally, I stood and blurted out, in what must have sounded like a threatening voice, to the commissioner, "Now listen very carefully, because I want to be absolutely certain you and your two cohorts don't misinterpret what I say . . ."

Obviously Byron was apprehensive about what I was going to say and attempted to stop me by pulling me back down. I turned to him and said, "You've got to let me finish."

"I've spent all the time I care to invest in this," I went on, looking the commissioner squarely in the eye. "It's evident that your minds are made up, and you have a right to make a decision, so there's nothing more we can accomplish here today."

The three men nodded in unison.

I then recapped what I believed was their position: "You

are telling me that UCC sells a security, and the only way for us to sell memberships in the state of Indiana is by registering our company as a broker and our salespeople as registered representatives. Am I correct in saying that before one more UCC membership can be sold, securities licenses must be obtained, and, in fact, we must make our offer to prospective members with a registered prospectus?"

"Your understanding is correct," the commissioner said.

"In ten minutes it will be four o'clock, so I intend to wrap this up very quickly," I continued. "Do you have $400 in your pocket?"

"W-what?" replied the commissioner, somewhat startled by the question.

"Do you have $400 in your pocket?" I repeated.

"W-well, no."

"Do the three of you," I questioned, "have $400 between you?"

Refusing to answer, the commissioner snapped, "You're out of order. Enough of these nonsensical questions."

"I'll even take a check," I replied.

"I said that's enough."

"I want you to understand something," I said in a calm voice. "When I walk out of this room, we're going to sell UCC memberships tonight, tomorrow, and every day that we can find people who want to buy them. Now, I intend to walk out that door in just a matter of minutes, and when I do, I'm going to sell a membership to the first person I come across in the hall. If I have to, I'll even lend him the money to buy one. And I'm going to sell as many as I can to anyone I come across in the halls of this building. I was hoping you had some money yourself to buy one, so I could sell one in your presence. Then we could see what you were planning to do with your so-called cease-and-desist order. If you want to do something about it to stop me, then go right ahead. But it's going to take more than what's sitting in this room to stop me. In fact, you should plan to use your entire legal budget, because I'm going to take you to court, and when I do, I'll make you out to be the biggest laughingstock that Indiana ever had in a state office."

The commissioner was flabbergasted. He and his two aides stormed out of the room into a private office. The hearing was over. Byron and I looked at each other in surprise. We weren't sure how to interpret the commissioner's reaction.

On the way home, Byron lectured me for two hours on how I had committed financial suicide. I disagreed with him and said that if I had to do it all over again, I would. I firmly believe it's my right as a United States citizen to engage in my business in all fifty states, and nobody has the right to deny me that opportunity.

It turned out that I did the right thing. UCC continued to sell memberships in Indiana, and to this day, nearly two decades later, we have never heard another word about that cease-and-desist order. Two years later, we did request that the state give us a disposition on it. We wanted to have the order wiped from the records because, as we expanded into other states, we were required to fill out forms asking, "Has your company ever been guilty or been accused of being guilty of any infraction of a securities law?" In spite of making a series of inquiries to the Indiana securities department, Byron was never able to get a satisfactory reply. No matter how much he pursued it, the state could never find any record of the cease-and-desist order. In time, we simply gave up on it as if the incident had never happened.

## Profit Is Not a Dirty Word

Knowing that our business is unconventional, I should not have been surprised when I was summoned to appear before a confused and angry bureaucrat (it's been so long ago, I can't remember what governmental department it was). I was cross-examined for nearly an hour, during which time I answered a series of questions and gave a complete explanation about what UCC did. He finally exclaimed, "Ah, so what you are telling me is that United Consumers Club makes a profit."

"That's right, sir," I said.

"Now if I understand everything correctly, your company does not make a profit on the merchandise, but on the sale of the membership."

"Absolutely right," I smiled.

"So what we have here is a scheme to make money," he said with a sinister smirk appearing on his face.

"Of course it's a scheme to make money. General Motors is also a scheme to make money. And so is the doctor when he performs surgery on your wife or mother. The doctor went to medical school, and now he's entitled to be paid for his services."

"What are you getting at?" he questioned.

"This is what free enterprise in America is all about. There are millions of businesses and professions in this country that are not charitable institutions and, to use your term, are positively schemes to make money. As far as I'm concerned, profit is not a dirty word in a democracy."

## Little People with Big Egos

Hardly any of us escapes an occasional scuffle with somebody with an ounce of authority who relishes throwing his or her weight around. Just the other day, I witnessed a postal clerk berate a sweet old lady who had not properly wrapped and addressed a package. Instead of cordially explaining the proper procedure to her, he talked down to her as if she were a child. The poor woman walked away confused and nearly in tears. When I finally approached the counter, the same clerk never even bothered to look up to serve me. For a few seconds I felt as though I were an invisible man. "Could I have a roll of 100 first-class stamps?" I asked.

Instead of acknowledging my request or, for that matter, my presence, he continued doing some minor paperwork that I'm sure he could have done during a slow time when no customers were waiting in line. I noticed two other clerks standing around who were engaged in small talk. "Would it be too much trouble for somebody to please sell me some stamps?"

Again I was ignored.

"I think the average American would be more sympathetic toward proposed increases in postage if you guys treated your customers with more respect," I said in a rather loud voice.

It took that remark to finally get a reaction from the postal worker, and the dozen or so people who were also impatiently waiting in line applauded me.

"Here's your roll of stamps, buddy," the clerk hissed.

It so happens that I understand some of the economics of the postal service and I personally know postal service employees who are dedicated civil servants. However, I have little patience with the ones who act with disrespect toward the public they serve. Talk about biting the hand that feeds you.

It's like the time I was running to catch a flight from Los Angeles to Chicago. As I approached the agent at the gate, the airplane's doors closed, and the gate was pulled away. Admittedly, I was five minutes late. Barely able to catch my breath after running down the long corridor, I handed my ticket to the agent. Pointing to the aircraft, I exclaimed, "That's my flight."

"No, it isn't," he answered. "You've already missed that flight."

"But I have to be in Chicago this evening," I blurted out.

"That's the last one today. You can catch the red-eye at midnight, and it'll get you into O'Hare tomorrow morning at two."

"Can't you put me on that one?" I pleaded. "I have an important dinner engagement tonight."

"Nothing I can do now, mister."

"Oh, yes, there is," I said, getting hot under the collar. "I think if you can make the effort to pick up that telephone *and tell the pilot who I am*, he'll let me board."

That got his attention, "Who are you?" he questioned.

"Damn it, I'm a *customer*, that's who," I shouted. "Now tell him you have a customer who wants to board the plane."

Obviously I caught him off guard because, with that, he telephoned the pilot and said there was one more customer at the gate. Sure enough, they allowed me to board. It's a shame that I had to resort to hardball tactics to get some service. The agent should automatically serve *anyone* who is a customer—not just somebody who demands service.

There's one whippersnapper from the Department of Labor

whom I'll never forget. This young man marched into our Highland, Indiana, showroom unannounced and acted as if he was about to slap a padlock on our front door. This particular club was the first to be company-operated, although we had already opened two franchises. It was located in a small strip shopping center, and from the outside looking in, a passerby wouldn't have the foggiest notion what business we were in. There was simply a sign with our name on it, and back then nobody knew United Consumers Club from Adam. Like all of our showrooms, the windows were draped because we don't display merchandise, as do retailers who want to attract window-shoppers.

The staff consisted of ten people, including a secretary, showroom personnel, and several salespeople. Also working there was my seventeen-year-old son Jack and one of his buddies. They worked after school and on Saturdays, mainly doing odd jobs. I happened to be at the club on this particular day and was in the office when a secretary nervously entered. "Mr. Gagan, there's an official from the Department of Labor in the showroom who insists on seeing you immediately."

Jokingly, I replied, "If any of those people from the government departments actually labors, I'd like to meet him. Please have him come in."

The man promptly identified himself as a Department of Labor inspector by flashing his credentials, giving me a quick FBI-style flip of his wallet. His flippant attitude was a real turnoff.

"What can I do for you?" I asked.

"I want to ask your employees some questions."

"Is there something wrong? Is there a complaint about us?" I inquired.

"I'm not sure if something's wrong or not. That's why I want to ask some questions," he snapped at me.

"Well, before you start asking questions," I said, "you'd better be sure about what you're doing because you're going to have to deal with my attorney."

"Look, mister," he said, pointing an accusing finger at me, "I didn't come here for any particular reason, but if you don't want to cooperate, I'll come back with a subpoena . . ."

"Don't rattle your saber at me," I said. "What possessed you to come in here in the first place?"

"Your sign," he said, "and the drapes . . ."

"So it wasn't a business call, was it? You simply wanted to satisfy your curiosity. What's that have to do with the Department of Labor? Nothing!" I said, answering my own question.

"I just want to ask some questions," he replied. "Find out about their hourly wages, if there's job discrimination in your employment practices. I could talk to them now, or I can come back later with the subpoena. What's your pleasure, Gagan?"

"What are you worried about?" I asked. "Are you concerned about us selling everything at wholesale prices? Are you wondering how we can do it at so much less cost than anyone else? I bet you think we can do it because we have alien labor making it for us at slave wages. OK, go ahead and ask your questions. You have my permission to talk to anyone you want."

With that, he made the rounds, asking all sorts of questions and appearing somewhat frustrated that he couldn't find anything wrong. When he finally headed to the storage room where my son was unloading, I couldn't help shouting to my secretary, "Quick, go down to the basement and tell those illegal immigrants to stop sanding and polishing and hammering until this guy leaves. If he finds them down there, we'll all wind up in jail!"

Our "friend" began drilling Jack and his buddy in great detail. "We just drive the van, and we unload boxes," they told him. "That's all."

"Where's the basement?" he shouted.

"Basement?"

"You heard me, where's the door to downstairs?"

"But there's no basement," Jack said.

In a fury, he stormed out the door and circled the building several times, searching for an entrance to what he imagined must have been a hidden basement. What's so funny is that the club was a one-story building with a cement floor on a slab. And this guy was frantically searching for a basement! He had the entire office staff rolling on the floor in hysterics. He must have been quite embarrassed when he finally figured out that there really wasn't a basement. We never heard from the guy again.

## Winning over Intimidation

In 1974 we opened a club in Michigan, and some months later the franchisee called me to discuss a problem he was having with the local Better Business Bureau. "We're in compliance with every local and state law," he sighed, "but still, every time a prospective member calls the BBB to inquire about us, it gives us a negative rap. How should I handle it, Jim?"

"Don't," I insisted. "Let me come up, and *I'll* talk to them. That's what the home office is here for."

As a side note, it's important to remember that in those days the Better Business Bureau was a franchisee itself. Back then, there was an actual parent company that opened BBB franchises in towns and cities across the country, and each was a profit-making business. A BBB franchise made its money by charging dues to its members. When a consumer called the BBB to inquire about a particular business, the odds substantially increased that a good word was said on its behalf if it was a dues-paying member. On the other hand, a nonmember business took a calculated risk that a derogatory remark would be made. What this all boils down to is that businesspeople were frequently coerced into joining the BBB out of fear that something negative would be said about a nonmember. In some instances, out-of-town companies were blackballed by the local competition! (Today there is no longer a national BBB, but only local organizations that are self-sustaining.)

The woman who ran this particular BBB franchise pulled no punches. No matter what I had to say about UCC, she attempted to shoot holes through it. For thirty minutes I put up with her objections to everything I said. She had two comebacks to whatever I told her: "That's no good" and "That can't work." In frustration, I finally threw my arms up in the air and declared, "I can see this conversation is going nowhere, and I have no intention of getting into an argument with you. However, before I leave your office I want to ask you one question, and then I'm out of here."

"Go ahead and ask your question," she said belligerently.

"Now you've read our literature, and I gave you a full explanation about UCC. Will you please tell me in plain English what it is you so adamantly oppose about this wonderful new idea I've just explained to you?" Two other UCC people were present, so I added, "I've got to know what's behind all of this, and it will go no further than this room. If you'd like, my two associates will leave, and you can tell me in private."

"I'm not ashamed to say how I feel in front of them," she said.

"So please tell us."

"Do you have any idea what will happen when your outfit comes to our city?" she said. "If it's successful and spreads across the country like you say your plans are, do you realize what's going to happen?"

"I think I do."

"Well, you don't," she continued. "I've been here for thirty years, and I know every merchant in town. Once your club is established here, everybody will buy only from it, and what's going to happen to those business owners and their employees? They'll all be out of business!"

"Do I understand you correctly?" I asked when she finished. "What you're saying is that UCC will not only replace the retail establishments in town but eventually, as we expand, all retailers across the country. If that happens, then there will be only one seller of merchandise in the United States, *and it will be UCC!*"

She sat back in her chair and remained silent. "My dear woman, what a tremendous, flattering idea you just proposed," I said. "Would you mind signing your name to a letter stating what you just said?" I asked.

"I'll do no such thing," she replied.

"Well, for the record, there's no worry about UCC putting any local retailers out of business, and I hope nothing said this morning has suggested it." I then went on to elaborate on several reasons why she had nothing to worry about. And I added, "You're telling me that you think we're the best thing to come down the pike for the American consumer. Your fear is that everyone will desert Sears, J. C. Penney, Montgomery Ward, and every other retailer and come join us."

Still she didn't say a word. "Now, are you sure you won't put down how you feel in writing?"

"Oh, no, I couldn't do that," she muttered.

"Now, let's get one thing straight," I told her. "Please feel free to say whatever you want to say about UCC when people call in to inquire. But it had better be true. Because, from time to time, members of our staff are going to make inquiries, and if you ever give negative information about us that's not true, or if the tone of your voice implies something negative, I'm going to take you to court. You can count on it, ma'am."

Before I left her office, my parting words were: "If you have any doubts about what I just told you, I recommend you check with some other Better Business Bureaus I've tangled with. They're going to tell you to report anything you want about the man, but make sure it's accurate, because if you don't, he's absolutely litigious. And, for your information, that means *I love to sue*."

I evidently made my point. From time to time, we did monitor this particular BBB, and while it was never flattering to us, it never made a derogatory remark either.

Fight back like a tiger whenever anyone tries to intimidate you. I refuse to allow anybody to take a swipe at us. I know in my heart of hearts there's nothing about UCC to shame me when I walk through the gates of heaven. Knowing this gives me the conviction to stand tall and never worry about confronting anyone who attempts to browbeat us.

## If the Ground You're on Is Solid, Don't Be Afraid to Defend It

In 1978, the Federal Trade Commission sent us a letter stating that it was investigating buyers' clubs in general, and UCC in particular. I passed the letter to my attorney, Byron Chudom, and he followed up on it. A few months later, a man and a woman came to our offices and identified themselves as FTC investigators. They asked to look at all UCC records as part of their investigation to find out whether we were in violation of any federal ordinances. I understood their concern. Since we began in 1971, several other buyers' clubs opened across the country, many of which were out-and-out rip-offs. So the FTC was doing a fishing expedition, and we were, unfortunately, assumed guilty by association.

After a few hours of questioning Byron Chudom and our accountant, the two investigators settled down in the accounting department and began the tedious process of looking into our files, searching to come up with something. When I got wind that they were in the building and asking a lot of ludicrous questions, I became annoyed. Not only were they costing me considerable money in legal fees and employees' time, but the nature of the questions was insulting. We had done nothing wrong, yet they were treating us as if we were operating a fly-by-night business. Furthermore, their witch hunt was damaging the morale of our new employees, who, I feared, might begin to wonder if we were guilty of some wrongdoing. I was offended, and to strike back, I did something I would later regret.

I grabbed my black leather pilot's flight bag, rushed into the accounting department unannounced and frantically said, "Excuse me everybody, but I've got to talk to Byron. Byron, most of the money is in this bag, and I'm on my way down to the bank to withdraw the rest. Remember now, we've got to get the hell out of here by tonight." With that, I dashed out of the room, leaving Byron there with the FTC investigators.

"I demand to know who that was and what's going on around here," the man said.

"Oh, that was Jim Gagan."

"Would you explain what that was all about?" the woman ordered. "Exactly what did he have in the bag?"

"Not in a million years could I explain that one," Byron grinned.

Although Byron told them it was just a gag, they insisted on a full explanation. That lasted about an hour, then Byron finally insisted they leave the premises.

Two months later we received a subpoena. It stated that we must bring in every record of every purchase made by and through UCC. Additionally, the FTC wanted the name of the club member who made each purchase and what price he or she paid. Byron informed them that it would take three trailer trucks to comply with such a request. He said, "You're welcome to come here and look at all of our files, but it's not possible for us to bring everything in." After several days of discussion, a compromise was reached. A hearing was scheduled, and we agreed to present them with computer printouts, which alone required two full-sized automobiles in which to haul everything to them. To persuade the FTC to settle for this material, I said a certified statement would be furnished affirming the printouts were 100 percent accurate. "If you find a single irregularity," I declared, "I'll turn the company over to the FTC, and I'll go fishing."

A one-day hearing was held at the federal court building in Chicago, and two carloads of computer printouts were carried into the room. A hearing commissioner and his two aides were then given the tedious task of sifting out whatever it was they were looking for. A security guard was posted at the door. Byron and his young partner, Steve Meyer, accompanied me, and the three of us answered every question they could throw at us. At four o'clock, the commissioner announced, "It's obvious that we can't finish this today. Leave your records here, and we'll go through them and get back with you."

I looked at Byron and Steve, and they obviously knew what I was thinking. Steve stood up and said, "Mr. Commissioner, we're not leaving a single item here. Everything we brought we will take with us."

"No, you won't," the commissioner replied. "As a matter of fact, I'm ordering you to leave it here. May I remind you that there is a guard at the door."

I asked for permission to confer with my attorneys, and after five minutes Steve continued, "If you insist on keeping our records, you may as well arrest us now. Because at five o'clock, this hearing is over, and we're walking out of here with our records. May I remind you, Mr. Commissioner, that the subpoena specifically stated that we must appear here on today's date from nine-thirty to five o'clock. We complied with the subpoena, and if you want to see our records again, you must issue another subpoena, and at such time we will bring them back again. But we are not going to allow you to keep them."

We stood our ground, and at five o'clock the three of us walked out with every computer printout sheet in tow. Steve Meyer, Byron's protégé, had obviously caught on to his mentor's style, and would take no abuse from these officials. To this day, Steve continues to represent UCC nationally.

For an entire year, we heard nothing from the FTC. Then one day we received a one-paragraph release issued by the FTC in Washington stating that while some buyers' clubs are dishonest, others are not, and the public should be aware of this when purchasing such memberships. And that was that.

To this day, my blood pressure rises whenever some trigger-happy bureaucrat decides to conduct a witch hunt and decent, conscientious businesspeople are victimized. Of course, these activities add an extra cost to doing business, which, in turn, companies must pass on to their customers. It's remindful of a merchant adding 5 to 10 percent to his retail prices for breakage and theft. It's bad enough for the vast majority of the public who are honest to bear these added costs, but when the federal government slaps such a burden on sincere, hard-working businesspeople, it's a disgrace!

## Don't Buck the System, but Walk Softly and Carry a Big Gun

To paraphrase Teddy Roosevelt, I believe in carrying a big

gun. I have never gone out of my way to purposely start a fight with anyone, let alone a government agency. But as you can surmise, neither do I back down from a fight. I've always abhorred bullies, and to this day I refuse to submit to their intimidation. It's a matter of principle. Every time somebody pushes a man or woman around, a piece of his or her self-esteem is whittled away.

Even though it might appear as if I like to buck the system, I believe in making every attempt to work within it. Today, there are UCC clubs across the United States, and by the mid-1970s, whenever we'd enter a new state, our standard procedure was to send a highly qualified lawyer to the state's attorney general's office and its consumers' affairs division. This was our way of formally introducing ourselves, and at these first meetings, our lawyer routinely submitted a listing that included every piece of paper we intended to use in the state, and we suggested they review our literature and keep it on file. We also listed references, some of which were from other state's attorney general's offices. As a matter of policy, we asked to be informed of any local or state statutes that we should know about, and if we were not in compliance, we would make necessary changes in our modus operandi to conform with state statutes.

As we expanded and gained more experience, it became necessary to obtain the services of Rudnick and Wolfe, a Chicago law firm that specializes in the field of franchising. Now, every year, Erik Wulff, a partner in the firm, monitors all legislation in every state in which UCC operates, and he makes sure that we comply with all applicable laws. The firm reviews all of our documents, including such things as finance and retail installment contracts, franchise agreements, and new members' booklets, to make certain we don't unknowingly violate a particular law. Additionally, we use the services of a lobbyist association in the states where UCC clubs exist, and we monitor all legislation that we feel will affect us.

When I opened our first franchises in Indiana, I didn't do these things, because I didn't know any better. UCC has come a long way since 1971. As far as I'm concerned, every ethical businessperson who complies with local and state statutes has a right as a United States citizen to engage in business anywhere in this great nation. Such an enterprise doesn't have to be profitable; all that is necessary is for it to be legitimate.

## Knowing When to Walk Away from a Fight

There are times when you can win a fight and still end up losing. Let me explain. In some instances, a corporation can be the victim of an overzealous prosecutor who attempts to use vague federal statutes to transform civil regulations into criminal law. There are countless federal, state, and local regulations that have been criminalized, meaning it's up to the prosecutor to decide whether criminal as well as agency action should be commenced. In recent months, the notorious RICO statute has been applied by government agencies to go after employees and companies in the banking and securities industries. Company officials in the energy and manufacturing industries have also felt the threat of criminal charges involving environmental violations.

Whether found guilty or not guilty, a company faces a difficult decision to determine whether it should fight or plead. Management must weigh the evidence on both sides of the case. It must decide whether prolonged and costly litigation in terms of money, time, diversion of company energies, and reputation exceeds the likely penalties of a guilty plea. So, under certain circumstances, you can't win even when you're innocent. Sometimes you must simply lick your wounds and walk away.

# —5—
# THE LINE IS DRAWN HERE

DURING UCC'S FIRST YEAR, I approached several mattress manufacturers to sell their products to UCC after I learned about the surprisingly large markups retailers make on mattresses. I liked that. Any time we could show the suggested retail price of an established, name-brand product priced considerably more than the wholesale price, the comparison made us look great. At a meeting with a well-known national firm's executive, she made a proposition that she thought I couldn't refuse. "Yes, UCC can carry our line."

"That's wonderful," I exclaimed, not concealing my enthusiasm, having noticed that a full queen set, with a suggested retail sticker price of $1,000, wholesaled for $375. "We'll sell 'em by the carload," I chuckled.

"We'll put your label right here," she smiled, pointing to one of the mattresses.

"We don't have a label," I said.

"Then we'll make one up for you. We'll make it in red, white, and blue, just like your logo," she continued. "This will work to your advantage because, with the high markup, you can make an extra $100 or so on each sale and still sell them for half the retail price."

"No, that's not the way our business works," I said. "We'll use your label, and we'll sell them without any markup."

"You can sell them for any price you want, Mr. Gagan, but you can't use our label. I'm sorry. It has to be yours. Otherwise, we'll take a lot of heat from our other dealers."

"I don't want to make *any* money selling mattresses."

"We'll be delighted to sign a contract with you, Mr. Gagan, but in it we will stipulate that your label must be on our products. That's the way it works."

"I am prepared to place a large order, ma'am, but only if it's with your brand name on the mattresses," I replied.

"Don't you think you can sell it with your name on it?" she asked.

"I'm sure we can," I answered. "But we're interested in adding your line because it's a prestigious name. Now, as I see it, you're telling me that, in essence, you're ashamed to do business with me, and that doesn't sit well with me."

"If I insulted you, sir, it was not intended," she apologized.

"Just the same, you did. You don't want your name associated with mine. Keep in mind, ma'am, that if you don't want to be connected with me, you are not going to be connected with my checkbook either."

"You're being very shortsighted," she said.

"If I were to handle your line, I'd be submitting to your extortion, and I won't do that."

"Don't you think you're going a bit too far?" she interrupted.

"Not in the least," I interjected. "If UCC were to sell your mattresses with our label, we'd still tell our members they were your products but with our name on them. There's no doubt that the majority would accept that. But the skeptics among our prospective members, as well as some of the existing ones, would say, 'I thought so. Now this guy is starting to make his own product. It's not going to be the same quality as the *real* Sealy or Serta or Bassett, and they're probably making it somewhere in Haiti. And what's more, I bet the bunting is filled with cholera-infested rags. Gagan's just telling us it's that brand. Who does he think we are?'

"I just gave you a worst-case scenario," I continued. "Most of our members would buy it without thinking twice, and they would be getting a terrific value. These people have faith in UCC. You're relying on their goodwill toward me because I have always kept my word with them. Now you're asking me to break my word."

"I beg your pardon . . ."

"That's right. We'd be giving them less than what they would get from your retailers. Other dealers sell your mattresses to their customers with your label on them; we would never consider giving our members anything less."

"Why don't you think about it, Mr. Gagan, and perhaps you'll see things our way," she said.

"I'll say just one more thing, ma'am, and I'm out of here," I said. "You'll never do business with UCC. You can mark my words on that."

Some people think I have a stubborn streak and that I should be more flexible. Personally, I think I am flexible, yet there are certain issues on which I won't give an inch. When I have to, I will bend. But on matters of principle, I draw the line. There is no compromise.

## Maintaining Your Standards

Standards must never be compromised. Suppose, for example, that the manager of a hotel told the staff, "As you know, I have always stressed cleanliness. But with the long holiday weekend coming up, we're booked for 100 percent occupancy, and we're extremely short-staffed. So, in order to clean all the rooms, for the next three days I want every housekeeper to clean for only two-thirds the amount of time you normally spend in each room. We're in a pinch, so do whatever you must do to cut corners. Now, by no means should anyone interpret this to mean that we are lowering our high standard for housekeeping. Beginning on Tuesday morning, it's back to the normal way we do things around here, and I'll expect each of you to resume your best housecleaning efforts again, so we may maintain our high standard."

It only takes one time for management to deliver such a speech, and forever after, workers are confused. The real message this manager signaled is that a double standard exists, and it's based on how management feels at a particular time. The real objective becomes lost, and once it is lost, it is lost forever. Employees no longer understand what management is trying to accomplish.

It's no different from setting a midnight curfew for a teenager. "Now, I want you in by twelve on the dot, and if you're not, you'll be docked for two weeks," a parent tells a child. However, when the child comes home at twelve-fifteen, not a word is said about it. Once a young person knows that the curfew can be disregarded, he or she doesn't understand what the real boundaries are. As a result, no matter what idle threats are later made, they have no meaning. The child can come home at any time.

On the other hand, a mother tells her daughter, "I want you home exactly at twelve o'clock this evening, and if you're home at one minute after midnight, don't expect to go out of this house for the next two weekends. Is that perfectly clear?"

"Oh, mom," the daughter moans, "all my friends' mothers let them come home at one."

"You heard me. Be home at twelve. End of conversation," the mother says firmly.

At three minutes past midnight, the mother hears the front door open. While she would certainly prefer to stay in bed, she gets up, puts on her robe, and goes downstairs to announce that the curfew has been violated.

"But, mom," her daughter cries, "it wasn't my fault. Tommy's watch was slow."

"No excuses, young lady. Don't you dare even think about going out for the next two weekends."

Children have no trouble understanding such messages. Once a parent compromises, however, there is going to be a disciplinary problem. As every parent knows, in the short run it's easier to turn his or her head and look the other way, but in the long run, the child becomes unmanageable. Most children will test a parent to see how far they can go. A caring and intelligent parent knows that the child is "testing" and wants to be disciplined—it's a sign that the parent loves the child. The child feels secure with this "tough love."

In my business, there is always the temptation to turn my head when a franchisee violates one of our rules. This is particularly true when one of our top-producing clubs steps out of line. Sure, there is a temptation to ignore it or act as if it's only a minor oversight. After all, no manager likes making waves with a top producer. For instance, a franchise owner sends a payment in late, or perhaps fails to properly complete a monthly report. To some, these are minor infractions to be taken lightly, but once someone is given even the slightest leeway to bend the rules, it's certain that person will do it again, and even more so the next time. Then, when the time finally comes to come down hard on the person, he or she is angry and bitter. Why? Because this person is confused. He or she wants guidelines.

The truth is, when a company sets standards that are maintained, it's a sign of strength. My franchisees want a strong UCC; their futures depend on it. This, too, is tough love. Our message to our franchisees is: "We will not allow you to continue to abuse your business and our business."

## Terminating the First UCC Franchise

One of the saddest and most frustrating times of my career happened in mid-1975, when I had to terminate the first franchise I sold. That's right . . . the guy from Anderson, Indiana, whom I sold on a napkin. I always took pride in the way I made that sale, and the man who bought the franchise was one of my longtime acquaintances. It went much further than sentimentality. For a while, it was a very profitable franchise that was also responsible for several innovations that became standard procedures for UCC.

The demise of the franchise was the result of a man falling victim to sudden wealth, a sickness I believe is more lethal than when somebody runs into tough times and things fall apart. When an individual's annual earnings rise from

$20,000 to $200,000, it can be even more difficult to survive than when they nosedive. Most people know how to tighten their belts when they face adversity, because they're programmed to deal with it from experience, but they have extreme difficulty adjusting to prosperity. With a sudden taste of affluence, they begin to indulge in their newly acquired habits, which may include luxury cars, country clubs, and yachts. Very quickly they are more interested in enjoying their newly found wealth than in doing what they did to earn the money to pay for their new toys. This is basically what happened to that fine franchisee in Anderson.

He got carried away with playing the role of executive instead of behaving like one. In short, his overhead skyrocketed because he was no longer simply content to operate a profitable franchise. He wanted to be a big shot. For example, not only was his private office five times larger than needed, it looked as if a Hollywood director served as his interior decorator. He had three telephone lines and a private secretary. While there is nothing wrong with these amenities, they're not necessary in our business and, in fact, tend to get in the way. The franchisee also published an expensive newsletter that was mailed to his club members. It was strictly an ego trip and contributed nothing but added overhead. As a result of the high lifestyle, he paid little attention to the nitty-gritty of the business, and sales production began to fall.

For months I rode herd on him, telling him to straighten up his act, but he was too caught up in "the good life" to pay attention. In hindsight, what ended up happening was predictable—he took money from members and failed to submit the money to us, in turn, to process with furniture manufacturers. While his intentions were only to "borrow" this money to pay his other bills, he was spending what did not rightfully belong to him. When somebody uses Peter's money to pay Paul, it's only a matter of time before it catches up with him.

In those days we weren't computerized, so it took a while before I was made aware of these shenanigans. By then, the franchisee was so deep in the hole, I had no choice but to terminate his contract. UCC had to absorb an $80,000 loss, which, back then, made a sizable dent in our bank account. But there was no choice. I hated to do it, but I had to let him off the hook; he would have been into UCC for even more money.

Even though I stopped the hemorrhaging in Anderson, it wasn't the only franchise that was getting deep into debt. There were several others that were also falling behind in what was due UCC. For the next two years, these problems continued to plague us, and even though we were selling a lot of new memberships, it was hurting our bottom line. Part of the blame was due to my friendships with our franchisees. In particular, I got too close to the guy in Anderson. I wanted so badly for him and the others to succeed that I allowed my affection for them to interfere with my business judgment. As a consequence, I failed to execute proper fiscal responsibility. In addition, I didn't abide by the terms set forth in contracts. Instead, I allowed my emotions to run the business, and it was not in the best interest of the company.

In short, I was trying to run a national organization based on my love and affection for my people. It was as if I were more concerned about winning a popularity contest than running an organization. Over the years, I've observed many other entrepreneurs make this same mistake. They get too close to their employees, and by doing so, they become too soft on their people. What's more, they commit the cardinal sin: they break the very rules that they established—good rules that should have been followed to the letter. As a result, their companies have no discipline, and they flounder. It's OK to love your people, but it has to be *tough love*.

## Black Thursday

It seems that every firm experiences a day when problems come to a head and demand immediate, often drastic action. If one day stands out as our most infamous, it is November 24, 1977, referred to at UCC as Black Thursday. I returned to the office that afternoon following a three-day trip to the West Coast, and I sensed something wasn't right. Fred Wittlinger, my right-hand man, whom I dearly love, was down in the dumps, which is totally out of character for an up person such as he is. We chatted for about fifteen minutes, and finally I came right out and asked him, "Fred, what's wrong? I've never seen you like this before."

"Oh, nothing, Jim," he said unconvincingly.

"Come on, Fred, I know you too well. What's bothering you?"

Not a man to complain, Fred remained silent, but within an hour, I was able to get it out of him. He was upset about an irate telephone call he had received from a franchisee, who happens to be one of the loveliest women in the world. To this day, she and her husband operate a franchise in Ohio and are absolutely delightful people. She, however, was upset because several members in their club were having fits about orders that had been placed for snowblowers but had not been delivered. The winter of 1976 had been one of the worst on record, and already the season was again shaping up to be a humdinger, so UCC was promoting snowblowers. Members were ordering them by the truckload, but our supplier was unable to ship them out fast enough to meet the demand, and tempers were flaring.

As a consequence, she and Fred, who are both normally cool and calm people, exchanged a few harsh words. The conversation ended when Fred cut her short and terminated the phone call. Fred is a real professional, and he was later ashamed about his behavior. Besides, this was a woman he liked and respected. Unfortunately, there was a lot of stress in the office at the time of her call, and her complaint was the proverbial straw that broke the camel's back.

The more Fred and I talked, the more upset I became. I quickly realized that his conversation with her was only the tip of the iceberg. This incident was just one of countless telephone calls from franchise owners that I viewed as having hostile overtones. Many calls were demanding; others were disrespectful. I asked Fred to pull out current franchise statements, because, frequently, looking at the numbers provides me with the general mood of the organization. I reviewed the statements and was appalled to observe that so many franchises had been withholding payments due UCC. Some were using the members' money that should have been set aside for merchandise. Although not to the same extent, they were doing exactly what led me to terminate the Anderson franchise.

By coincidence, my reason for returning that day was to attend a franchisee meeting on Saturday. My plans called for me to deliver a pep talk, but after speaking with Fred, I decided there was something more important to say. I asked my secretary, Armina Thorpe, to request that every manager in the building come immediately to my office to hear an important announcement. When they assembled, I reviewed the snowblower incident with them and mentioned how I understood it was not an isolated affair. Heads began to nod. I also showed them the sad state of affairs that appeared on our financial statements: approximately $700,000 in back fees was due us—outrageously high based on the sales volume of memberships at the time.

"Cancel the entire agenda set for Saturday's meeting," I insisted. "The meeting will start as usual in the morning. Just serve breakfast, and then I want the microphone turned over to me. I'll take it from there."

Everybody knew something was up, because it was not my style to run a full-day meeting. Furthermore, several speeches had already been prepared by other managers, and now I was shelving them because I had a more important message. I was also visibly upset, and as I spoke, I made no attempt to hide it.

It was Black Thursday all right, but nothing compared to how black that Saturday promised to be. I spent all day Friday with the office door shut, dictating a speech to Armina. This, too, caused more speculation, because, first, my office door is rarely closed and, second, I never have a written speech. I only use a few notes and speak extemporaneously. "Armina, I want this speech typed double-spaced in bold print because I intend to read it word for word. And one more thing. Absolutely nobody else is to read it."

When I was through, Armina shook her head. "I can't believe it," she said.

"I would like you to be present on Saturday morning, too," I said.

The meeting was held at a local restaurant in Schererville, Indiana, across the street from our home office. Every UCC franchise owner and all key UCC managers were present. Prior to addressing the franchisees, I read my speech to Fred Wittlinger, Jack Allen, and my son Jack. It put them in a mild state of shock. "This is how it has to be said," I told them.

My speech lasted half an hour, which is too long a text to include, so the following is a synopsis:

> It should come as no surprise to anyone present here today that the current condition of United Consumers Club, Inc., is not what any of us desires it to be. This morning, I intend to examine the symptoms that plague us as well as the underlying causes, so that they can be dealt with directly and honestly.
>
> The severity of these problems is so staggering that unless we are able to find acceptable and practical solutions, we will witness the demise of the United Consumers Club. I am well aware of the harshness of my statement, so listen carefully. We have worked very hard to build something wonderful and exciting, and we have seen UCC grow, beginning with one man with an idea, to an extraordinary organization. During our first six years, we have succeeded far beyond what outsiders ever believed was possible. But I am not here to dwell on past achievements. Something has since happened, and it saddens me to inform you today that the wonderful magic we once had has vanished. This is a harsh reality that we must face, and it is why I am addressing you today. I will elaborate.
>
> In 1971, UCC was founded with a dream to bring the consumer closer to the manufacturer. Most people said it could never be done. Since then, in only six short years, we have won the admiration and respect of consumers, manufacturers, and bankers. We provided an honest, profitable marriage that is good for all parties—the consumer,

the manufacturer, and the UCC employee. In the process, we made believers out of many skeptics. Yet, in spite of our progress and knowing now that UCC can accomplish what it set out to do, something now is missing that threatens our very existence. Gone are the enthusiasm and magic of believing that each of us once had. We no longer function as a team, and as a consequence, we are self-destructing.

I am not blind. I know what opinion franchisees have of the national parent company and its staff. You believe your president is neurotic, bordering on psychotic. You think I am a dictator with little concern for problems that are present in your clubs. You further believe that the officers of this organization are incompetent and have no understanding about the problems prevalent in the field. All in all, you feel a lack of leadership and that we have let you down. Harsh words? Perhaps . . . but truly spoken.

Now let me tell you what the staff at headquarters thinks about you. You are uncompromising ingrates who look only for fault and, in fact, seem to thrive on having an unblemished record for your inability to give even an ounce of credit to the home office people who support you. As far as I'm concerned, you are the biggest bunch of ingrates who ever occupied this earth since Adam bit into the apple. He was in paradise until he bit the apple. You make Adam look like a conservative. When your business is running smoothly, you're eager to accept all the kudos. You obviously believe your accomplishments have been made in spite of the antagonism and incompetence of the parent corporation.

Let's look at who you really are. You don't do your paperwork properly, and it causes chaos in processing your orders. You are people who, when things are difficult, can't pay your bills, and when things are good, won't pay your bills. Among you there are those who lie about sales, hold back royalties, and never stop demanding more and more services for less and less royalties.

Sounds unattractive, doesn't it? It is a sad commentary, and I assure you this is not the way UCC was ever envisioned by any of us, staff or field, who once took a pledge that fidelity, brotherhood, and love would be our trademark. Now instead of pulling together, we are bickering and pulling apart. Certainly the UCC house divided is proving the old adage that it cannot stand.

From this moment on, the fate of the United Consumers Club rests entirely in the hands of the people assembled in this room this morning. Whether we go forward and recognize the bright future we all had once envisioned will be decided today. We know today that what we dreamed about in 1971 is no longer a dream. The club works, if you work at it. There is not a single record of a failure among our franchises—people have failed, but our marketing concept is a proven success. If UCC is to cease as an entity, it will not be the end of what we have pioneered. It will only mean that we have failed, but what we have started will not be in vain. Other buyers' clubs will surely follow in our footsteps. What we have started is far bigger than any of us as individuals.

I want you to listen very carefully to what I have to say now, because your careers are riding on it. I refuse to have this company continue doing business with people such as yourselves, whom I don't feel are giving UCC a fair shake. Things are going to have to change, and I want changes to begin immediately. Here's what's going to happen: My staff and I are leaving this meeting for a two-hour lunch. Then we will come back, and I want all of you to have collectively put into writing five good reasons why this company should continue.

Because many of you are late in your fees, in order for UCC to remain in business, it has become necessary for me to personally sign for three-quarters of a million dollars. Frankly, at this moment, I don't think I should subject myself to such a risk. After all, I'm doing it to finance the debt you owe me. So unless you can give me five solid reasons why UCC should continue, this organization is history.

With those final words, I walked out of the meeting with my staff following me. We refused to talk to any of the franchisees. We went to a restaurant down the road for lunch, and although nobody joined me for a midday drink, I had a scotch and soda and a big cheeseburger, followed by coffee and a cognac. I was with a very glum group of executives whom I felt needed some consoling.

"I don't want any of you to worry. We have been honest with our franchisees. We have never cheated anyone, and what I said to them today was the most honest thing of all. We faced our problem, and this is half the solution. Now we will go back, and it's up to them. Unless they can dig themselves out of the hole they've put us is, we have no alternative but to terminate every franchise."

Those people who had been with me for a while knew that once I draw the line, I won't budge. That's where I will fight to the death. Nobody said a word at lunch. They knew I meant what I said, so there was nothing to discuss.

When we returned to the meeting, I walked to the podium and said, "What's it going to be?"

Somebody stood up and said that they had collectively put together the list I had requested. "That's fine," I replied. "Write them on the blackboard."

Five statements were listed:

1. We will pay all of our back bills to UCC within one year.
2. We will work with you instead of against you.
3. We will do our paperwork properly.
4. No direct calls will be made to suppliers, but instead we will contact the company when there are problems.
5. No complaints of members will be referred to the home office, but will instead be handled by the local club manager and appropriate UCC staff person.

There was a look of relief on the faces of my staff, but I wasn't about to make it too easy for the franchisees. "Your five statements are fine if this is what is truly going to occur," I said, "but based on past performances, I have no reason to believe you'll perform. I want some assurances from you."

"What assurance do you want?"

"I recommend that you form a committee to serve as some

sort of vigilante service. This way, when I have a problem with a particular troublemaker, I can relay it to the committee, which, in turn, can contact that franchisee and straighten it out. Each of you must realize that when one club drags its feet, it could potentially take every franchise down with it. From now on, I want to see everyone working together as a team. I don't want to ever have to talk to you again like I did today."

As far as I'm concerned, we came of age on that day. It marked a major turning point in the history of this company—UCC became a business rather than an emotional experience. While the main event happened on a Saturday, it was on Black Thursday that I decided to lay down the law. It all started because of a snowblower.

Most entrepreneurs have their own Black Thursday. But there comes a time when they must grab the bull by the horns and lead their people, rather than just hope everyone will somehow work together. A strong leader has to lead, and although the leader's decisions may not always be popular ones, they do serve the best interest of the organization. In time, others will follow his or her lead. People welcome this form of strong leadership, and they need it.

## The Tail Doesn't Wag the Dog

In the late 1970s, the top UCC club was based in Lakeland, Florida. It was operated by two partners, as unlikely a pair of characters as I've ever met (one, whom I'll call Mutt, was 5'4" tall, and the other, whom I'll refer to as Jeff, was 6'8" tall). For a while, they went like gangbusters, and, by 1981 were operating three clubs and signing up in excess of two hundred members each month. They also generated more than $300,000 in annual royalties for UCC. But the more business they submitted to us, the more trouble they caused. They were rude to our office staff and literally went out of their way to be disagreeable.

During a national UCC conference held in Orlando in 1979, Mutt and Jeff and their key people acted as if they came to rock the boat. In addition to being disrespectful to management, they belittled other franchisees and ridiculed our speakers. Our home office staff had tipped me off that some friction had been brewing for six months, but I never imagined they would behave so inappropriately at a national conference. I had thought that, as our top franchise, they would set a positive example, but instead they were a liability.

Jeff approached me after the first day and said that he and his partner, Mutt, and their two key lieutenants wanted to have a private meeting with me. I agreed but insisted that several members of my staff accompany me. I invited their wives to attend, too.

We gathered in a meeting room at the hotel, and I asked them what they wanted to discuss. "We like the business," one of them said, then proceeded to say what they didn't like about it. They were not pleased with how we managed our end of it, and I asked for suggestions on where we should improve. A few meager recommendations were made. Then one of them said, "What we really want to talk to you about today is money." I quickly realized that everything else had been a smokescreen. *Now* we'd get to the nitty-gritty. "OK, so talk about money," I said.

"We've done a big job for UCC, haven't we?"

"Yes, you have," I agreed.

"We plan to do an even bigger job. So far, we've just scratched the surface."

"That's terrific," I smiled.

"Well, as we expand, we'll make even more royalties for UCC."

"That's fine with us," I interrupted again.

"We think that the amount of money we're paying UCC is too high, and we should pay a lower royalty than the other franchises because of our volume."

"What are you suggesting?" I asked.

"Here's the crux of it. We want a reduction in royalties."

"I'm sorry, but I don't know what you mean," I said, somewhat surprised. "How can we do that?"

"The more members we sign up, the less royalties we should pay," one blurted out.

"I want to back this up," I interjected. "You're saying that the more members you have, the less you should pay UCC for servicing them?"

"Well, that's one way to look at it," one spoke up.

The other joined him: "Eh, yeah, that's right."

"So if you pay $x$ royalties per new membership, it will drop down in half if you increase your production from 200 to 400, and even more at 500, and so on. Is this what you mean?"

The four men and their wives nodded their greedy heads in unison.

"Let's then carry this illogical premise to a logical conclusion," I said. "If you sell 1,000 memberships, you won't have to pay me anything a year. And I will service them free for you because you sell so many. Is this what you suggest?"

"We didn't mean . . ."

"Of course, you did. Let's look at it further. We have some other top franchises that are producing in your neighborhood, so should we do the same with them? If we do, how can we afford to give good service to our members as the size of UCC continues to increase? And the larger our business grows, and the more service it requires, the less we receive for our work. Or do you recommend that only your clubs pay a lower rate and we do it surreptitiously?"

"Well, yeah, you might have to cut the royalties with every franchise," they agreed.

"I don't think you people have a clear understanding of our business. Do you realize that once you sign a member, UCC must service all future orders, and we don't make one red cent from those transactions? Your club sends the exact cost of the merchandise to us, and we make no profit on the transaction. Now you can't believe that we don't incur a cost for what we do."

"That's your problem," Jeff said. Mutt's face lit up as if I were put in a corner from which I could not get out.

With that, I stood up, and my parting words were: "Nobody, not you or anyone else, tampers with this company. From today forward, my advice to you is that you had better shape up and get with the program. And, you [addressing Mutt], of all people, were the one who came to me when you were broke. How soon you forget how I carried you, and now that your club is thriving, you have the gall to tell me I don't deserve to get paid what's due me. Unless you conform and do things exactly by the book, you can kiss this business good-bye." There was nothing more to be said; my entourage and I walked out of the room. The Lakeland group attended the conference's affair that night, but not a word was mentioned about what had been said that afternoon.

It was only a few months later that they sent a letter to UCC stating that they were terminating their contract and starting a buyers' club of their own in Lakeland. In turn, we sent a letter to the members that we would continue to serve them and, in fact, opened a new facility to service them. Mutt and Jeff's greed finally got the best of them. To generate additional revenues, they started selling gold stocks, gold bullion, and coins. It was a rip-off, and the beginning of the end for them. Nine months later, *their* club folded, and they each filed for personal bankruptcy.

### Showdown in Palm Beach

Another of our largest franchises was run by two brothers who were based in West Palm Beach. They operated three clubs and generated monthly royalties paid to UCC in the $25,000 range. These brothers were very independent and, no matter how much money they made, were always working against us. Once again, it was a matter of being driven by greed. After all, their personal incomes were several times higher since joining UCC. In 1982, they began charging every new member an extra $100 for a membership in a car club. It wasn't even an option—the $100 fee was automatically included as an add-on to the UCC membership fee. They lined up several dealers in the Palm Beach area, who, in turn, sold cars anywhere from $100 to $400 over invoice. On the side, the dealers paid them a piece of what they made on the sale. In addition, they operated a food club that sold groceries to their members, also at a profit.

From day one, we considered it sacrilegious to sell to our

members at any price above wholesale. I have always preached that, by violating this doctrine, we would prostitute ourselves, and our credibility would go down the drain. Furthermore, there are no exceptions; every club must uniformly abide by this rule. So, naturally, when I first learned that our West Palm Beach franchise had its own car club going, I personally paid them a visit to tell them to cease and desist at once.

As it turned out, I discovered that it was just the tip of the iceberg. Only then did I find out they were selling food, too. To my chagrin, I discovered they had suppliers other than those with which UCC worked, and they were making a markup on the merchandise sold through these sources. I told them to stop immediately. They refused, telling me that there was nothing in their contract that prohibited them from their side businesses. In effect, they were under the erroneous impression that they were making so much money for UCC that we would turn our back and allow them to continue. "Either clean it up and do it our way, or get out!" I insisted. They had made so many phony promises to their members, they were unable to straighten out their act and consequently elected to go off on their own.

The contract's noncompeting restrictive covenant is quite specific and prohibited them from operating a club in the same area on their own. We took them to court. The court ordered each brother to pay $75,000 to UCC. In a short time, their club folded, too.

## Eliminate the Troublemakers

There are some people who will always fight the system. They want to cause waves. I'm not opposed to change; I'm all for it—as long as it's change for the better. But some individuals aren't interested in improvement. They only want to make change for the sake of change, and that's not progress.

We often refer to UCC as a family, and even the best of families have their squabbles. There's nothing wrong with having differences; indeed, it would be a very dull world if we all agreed on every subject. There are certain issues, however, on which an organization must think in harmony, when all members of the team must have the same objectives and move in tandem. This doesn't mean there can be no room for individuality and independence. In fact, our franchisees are independent businesspeople. Still, in a franchised business, there must be basic uniformity and consistency.

Every now and then a maverick joins our organization who attempts to buck the system. I'm somewhat of a maverick myself, so I don't think being a nonconformist is an undesirable trait. In fact, leading corporations like IBM often refer to their free-thinkers as "wild geese." Every organization needs some of these individuals. I just like our wild geese to fly in the same general direction as the company. I'm always willing to listen to new ideas and suggestions, but what I don't want are iconoclasts who always take a diametrically opposed position. We've had our share of these agitators in Lakeland and West Palm Beach, as well as a few others, and it's people like this who take the fun out of the business. I have discovered that the troublemakers represent about 25 percent of the nonconformists in an organization, and they're the ones who must be let go. They sap the energy of management and, even worse, demoralize the rest of the organization.

I recall when Photomat, the first quick photo company to provide fast service in shopping centers and malls, was a thriving enterprise. A few of its franchisees ganged up on them and caused so much trouble that the company finally went out of business.

Years ago, there were a few dissident UCC franchisees who tried to organize an association, which I thought would be destructive for UCC. When the dissidents approached our loyal franchisees, who represented the majority, they refused to join.

Some of the loyal ones called to inform me they were against having an association. One made the analogy to a labor movement attempting to unionize a company's work force. "When management treats its employees well, there is no need for a union," he said.

I wasn't about to sit on my thumbs while a handful of troublemakers tried to rock the boat. I called each of them individually and flew them in to the home office for private one-on-one meetings. Then I gave them an ultimatum. "Either run your club by the book, or you will lose your franchise." I didn't pull any punches, and everyone clearly understood that I meant what I said. Afterward, most of them straightened up, and I terminated the ones that didn't. To this day, there is not a franchise association. The franchisees know I'm against one, so nobody even brings the subject up anymore.

## The Short-Lived Vitamin Venture

We're constantly searching for new products and services to provide to our club members, and every year we add new suppliers. It's a matter of never wanting to stand still, in a constant effort to improve. In 1982 a decision was made to investigate the popular health and fitness field. Our studies revealed there was a high margin of profit on vitamins, which, in turn, would mean that by offering these products to our members, we would be giving them substantial savings. Along with Fred Wittlinger and my son Jack, I went to La Costa, the famous spa in La Jolla, California, to learn more about its successful vitamin program. Through a contact we made there, we met with a doctor on the staff of Scripps Institute in San Diego. Later we conferred with a packaging firm recommended by the spa people.

I had personally been taking vitamins for several years and was paying $41 a month for a regimen that contained a variety of required ingredients that supplemented my diet. I've always found it cumbersome, especially due to my hectic schedule that demands many meals away from home. With this in mind, we devised a convenient package that contained a box design with a supply of thirty small, attractive tinfoil-wrapped boxes to be used each day of the month. Each box contained four multiple-vitamin pills. These boxes were wrapped for freshness and, most importantly, for convenience.

In short, it was easy for a busy person to put the package in his or her pocket each morning and take vitamins at mealtime. Our vitamins would be priced at $8 to $10 a month versus $40 to $50 for comparable products on the market.

Through our contact at Scripps, we developed a wonderful product and invested heavily in advertising materials, brochures, and design, which included packaging with a description of the product. Our next step was to seek a manufacturer to produce the vitamins according to our formula. After we had met with several independent companies, a contract was signed with a New Jersey firm. This company agreed to make our line exactly to our specifications.

We were so enthusiastic about the vitamins that we decided to form a subsidiary company, complete with our own labels, called Club Products. In addition to selling this line in our clubs, our franchises would market them to retail outlets and nonmembers. By distributing Club Products to other sources, we could earn extra profits. It was a new venture for UCC— the first products bearing our name. Club Products was heralded as another major breakthrough for UCC. We made a major presentation to our franchisees at our May convention in 1983 and announced that the Club vitamins would be available later in the year. We invited a renowned nutritionist to be our guest speaker. The reception was terrific. Our franchisees were chomping at the bit.

Between the packager and the manufacturer, a series of delays occurred, and the line was finally shipped to us in early 1984. At last, everything looked as if it were a go. However, the person on our staff responsible for the new product said to Fred, "I think we ought to check to make sure the ingredients are as we originally specified." It was agreed that if we put our name on it, it had to be 100 percent of everything we claimed it to be. We wanted to be sure it was what our literature proclaimed. We wouldn't tolerate any margin of error, so we had to get a second opinion.

We hired an independent laboratory in Chicago to do an analysis of our vitamin line to determine every component in each pill. This company was one of the two biggest assaying laboratories in the United States, so we felt comfortable that we would be able to determine exactly what ingredients our vitamins contained. To our grave disappointment, the assay came back reporting our formula had not been used correctly. The actual product had less potency in several areas than was mandated by the formula designed especially for us.

In the meantime, the product line had already been shipped to UCC clubs. Fred, Jack Allen, and I personally placed calls to everyone and told them to ship everything back to the company at once.

"But we love the line," they said, "and our directors are all set to go with it."

"It's not what the label says it is, so we have to abort the line. Send it back and we'll give you a full refund."

My next call was to the manufacturer, and I told him what the assay reported. He had the gall to deny his company had done anything wrong. "That's totally asinine," I shouted. "I'm looking at an assay from one of the biggest labs in the country, and you didn't make what we contracted for. Now I'm going to have my staff determine the exact amount of money we've invested in this project, and I expect you to make good on it." He refused, and after a six-year court battle, a New Jersey court awarded us our costs plus interest.

With the enthusiasm our sales organization displayed, I am sure we would have succeeded in the vitamin business, but I refused to compromise on the product line. To this day, I think our short-lived vitamin venture was a good idea; we just got involved with the wrong manufacturer. But it left a bad taste in my mouth, and I didn't want to pursue it any further. Our game plan today is to stick to what we do best: the buyers' club business.

## Lightness of Foot

I am the sole stockholder of UCC, and thus far I have chosen to have this company remain a privately owned corporation. At this stage I don't want partners or other owners, because I have a single-mindedness of purpose about what is good for this company, where it is going, and how it will get there. It's my ball game. Not only do I own the bat and the ball, I own the ballpark. This ownership gives me the right to draw the line anywhere I think is in the best interests of this company. This doesn't mean I don't delegate, nor does it imply I don't rely on our executives to make major decisions. It does, however, mean I have the absolute right to unilaterally do what I believe is best for the company, and unless somebody can convince me that I am wrong, we do it my way.

It doesn't matter what the business is; during the start-up years, an entrepreneur must maintain absolute control of his or her company. This control makes it possible to realize swift decision making, an invaluable advantage that a sole proprietor enjoys. Of course, as a company expands, its growth rests on how well its owner can delegate authority to others.

# —6—

# SHORT-TERM SACRIFICES
# BEGET LONG-TERM GAINS

A TITLE I CONSIDERED FOR THIS BOOK was *How to Be an Overnight Success . . . in Twenty Years or Less*. Although I've heard about overnight successes, I've yet to meet one. I think it's more myth than fact, promoted in part by movies, books, and motivational seminars. Of course, there are a lot of dreamers in this world who choose to believe in fairy tales. In reality, though, there are few overnight successes.

Another fallacy is the keeping-your-nose-to-the-grindstone myth, which also doesn't guarantee anyone a one-way ticket to fat city. If so, all those who work for thirty years at a particular job would be rich. The world is full of such individuals who have nothing to show for their mundane existences except a long string of broken dreams. Neither do such attributes as knowledge and skill assure affluence. As Calvin Coolidge said, "Nothing is more common than unsuccessful men with talent . . . unrewarded genius is almost a proverb . . . the world is full of educated derelicts."

By no means do I scoff at hard work, knowledge, and skill, for these attributes certainly play a role in achievement. Each is definitely part of the success equation, but success can be achieved only when yet another vital ingredient is included: *one's willingness to make short-term sacrifices*. I believe this attribute is so essential to success that this entire chapter is dedicated to the proposition that without short-term sacrifices, long-term gains are doomed.

## A Quick Study of Japanese Long-Term Thinking

It should be no news to anyone that the Japanese economy has outperformed the United States economy in recent years. Consider the fact that no nation in the history of civilization had been so devastated as had Japan during World War II. Following the war's end in 1945, it took more than a decade for Japan to rebuild from the rubble, and still, throughout the 1950s, the country remained weak, and its people endured severe hardship. Yet, only a quarter of a century later, Japan's economy emerged as a superpower. This resurrection is undoubtedly the economic miracle of the twentieth century.

I believe every American can learn a valuable lesson by observing Japan's recovery and its subsequent rise as a leader in the world marketplace. To best realize how this phenomenon transpired, it is essential to understood the Japanese culture. I will begin by defining the word *mottainai*, which means, "All things are precious, and to waste is a sin." In America, we have no such word. Until recently we didn't think we needed one. The contrasts in our cultures are striking, and for good reason. Japan is a land of limited resources, and the United States is a land of plenty. We are a country that has evolved into a disposable society.

Because of immense shortages in both natural resources and real estate, the Japanese think, live, and work differently. Japan is terribly overcrowded with a population of 122 million who occupy a land about the size of California. Because of its jagged, mountainous terrain, only 17 percent of Japan is habitable. Its population density of 318 people per square kilometer is fifteen times greater than the United States' and three-and-one-half times that of China. With nearly half as many people as we have, its citizens live in an area about one twenty-fifth the size. (To look at it another way, if Japan today had the same population density as ours, there would be only eight million Japanese.) Japan has almost no raw materials except water. It is 99.7 percent dependent on other nations for oil imports; 100 percent for aluminum, iron ore, and nickel; over 95 percent dependent for copper; and more than 92 percent dependent for natural gas. Sony's chief executive officer, Akio Morita, has said, "We Japanese feel that all things are provided as a sacred trust and actually are only loaned to us to make the best use of. . . . We Japanese are obsessed with survival."

The awareness of space, or the lack thereof, has been deeply ingrained into the Japanese culture. By the early 1600s, Japan was already overcrowded, with a population density almost twice that of the present-day United States.

It is no wonder that the Japanese plan their lives with an eye fixed on the future. This thinking is evident in all walks of life in Japan. For instance, the average Japanese puts about 20 percent of his or her disposable income each year into savings. This figure is the highest rate of personal savings of any major nation, running about four times as high as what the average American saves. Then, too, the Japanese place a high priority on education. The functional adult illiteracy rate runs at less than 2 percent in Japan, compared to nearly 30 percent in the United States. Japan's best-educated and most capable young people are likely to seek a position in government, in contrast to the United States, where there is more interest in the private sector.

Today, billions are spent in energy research and development by Japanese industry and government, in contrast to the United States, where energy projects have been shelved as oil prices have fallen. Japan's crisis mentality is geared to preparation for a time when another energy crisis will arise. Its government's policy is based on giving research and development a long lead time and is not influenced by the short-term abundance of low-cost energy.

High personal savings, educational excellence, duty to country, investment in research and development—adherence to these doctrines demonstrates a deep concern about the future. Today's sacrifice and commitment build strong tomorrows.

Interestingly, today's Japanese are known throughout the world for the quality products they produce. For centuries, an emphasis on quality has been deeply instilled in their cultural heritage. In a land where natural resources are scarce, products must be made to endure, because they are not easily replaceable. It is true that for a decade or so following World War II, Japan produced inferior, shoddy products. During those years, there was no alternative, because of a lack of technology and supplies. But as Japan rebuilt, it did so with an emphasis on gradual and continual improvement. To this day, the Japanese maintain a philosophy of constant improvement.

In a nation bursting at its seams, Japan is said to be the world's most competitive marketplace. The Japanese companies that succeed are the ones that are the most service-oriented. Providing exceptional service is not an option in Japan; it's a prerequisite to attracting and keeping customers. It's a matter of survival; those companies that provide exceptional service are the ones that prosper. As American industry gears itself to enter a worldwide marketplace, those companies that survive in the twenty-first century will also be service-driven. As in Japan, it will no longer be an option.

It has been said that the Japanese are the most adaptable people in the world. During the late 1940s and through the 1970s, they emulated Americans with a passion. They took the best from us and other peoples around the world, and through borrowed bits and pieces, modern Japan emerged to become a world economic leader. The Japanese were not too proud to borrow ideas, refine them, and later claim them as their own. By doing so, Japan became a great industrial power in a period of thirty years or so. There is much that Americans can learn from the Japanese. I only hope that we don't allow false pride to stop us from gaining some valuable lessons from these remarkable people. After all, the Pacific is a two-way ocean.

## Having Direction

I can't imagine anyone beginning a new business or starting a new career without having a long-term goal. To do so is like starting on a long trip without a road map. Without direction, a person is likely to drift continuously without ever getting anywhere.

Did you ever get up on a weekend morning and have nothing planned for the day? On such occasions, you read the newspaper, watch some television, talk on the telephone, putter around, and by the end of the day, you haven't accomplished a single thing. As a result, you're apt to feel groggy and somewhat depressed. While you can't quite put your finger on why you feel this way, it's because you've wasted one full day—and one that you will never be able to recapture. Sadly, there are some people who drift for days, weeks, months, even years like this. They lack goals and, consequently, never achieve anything.

The down mood that comes from lacking direction is the inverse of that joyful feeling one has after putting in a productive day's work. When I have a list of things to do and *do them*, whether it's at my office or at home on the weekend, I'm euphoric with a sense of accomplishment at the end of the day. Of course, these are very short-term daily goals, so the thrill that comes from fulfilling a long-term goal is even more intense. Whether it's the birth of a baby, a graduation, or the closing of a major business deal, there's a tingling sensation that makes all the sacrifice worthwhile.

Having direction programs you to succeed. Once you make a commitment to a definite objective, the need to realize its accomplishment becomes entrenched in your subconscious. When this occurs, it's as if a little voice constantly guides you to move in the right direction. Anytime you stray from your objective, this little voice whispers, "Don't do that. It will keep you from reaching your goal. Instead, do this . . ." Once you become programmed to achieve your goal, you will find yourself automatically doing those things that will make it happen. Without a goal, you will drift aimlessly, and only by rare chance will you stumble upon someplace where you will find contentment.

## A One-Brick-at-a-Time Philosophy

Every long journey begins with the first step. Football games are won one play at a time, books are written one sentence at a time, and great buildings are built one brick at a time.

While it's vital to establish long-term goals, you must not look too far into the future and, as a result, neglect the present. To quote an old adage, "Rome wasn't built in a day." When I first began UCC, I did so with the vision of someday building a national organization. However, I knew that to accomplish my grand objective, I would need to first complete many little missions.

From time to time, an individual wants to join UCC and immediately own a franchise. While it is perfectly understandable that someone aspire to have his or her own club, unless this person learns the basics of our business, the odds are greatly stacked against him or her making it. At UCC, the basics begin with setting up an appointment on the telephone to giving a tour. At McDonald's it's called "grill time." Nobody can buy a McDonald's franchise without first spending some time behind the grill so he or she has hands-on experience with this aspect of the business. In Japan, newly hired executives are required to spend several weeks on the plant floor in order to gain an understanding about the work done by the people they will someday be managing. I don't care what business you're in. You must learn the basics.

I believe, however, there is a point where some companies overdo it by demanding that their executives work at labor positions for unnecessarily long periods. For instance, while I understand the importance of standing behind a hot grill to learn certain aspects about the hamburger business, there is only so much to learn by labor of this nature. Likewise, a candidate for middle and upper management employed by a manufacturing firm can only tighten so many bolts and nuts on an assembly line before the usefulness of such on-the-job training begins to wear thin. At UCC, we are aware of the need for potential franchisees to understand every facet of a club's operation, but we recognize when the point of diminishing returns is reached.

## Paying the Piper

Sooner or later, everyone who wants success badly enough must pay the piper. This includes entrepreneurs and corporate managers, athletes and students, writers and actors, and so on. While one individual may invest large sums of money in a start-up business, another may have a relatively small financial investment but devote long hours of sweat and toil to the job. This is not to suggest that a new business venture requires one in lieu of the other. Both capital and hard work are commonly required. However, while accumulating wealth requires an investment, it can be in the form of time and effort. I look at the investment of time as if a person were dealing with a bank offering very limited funds to borrow. The funds are those 1,440 minutes in every 24-hour day that each of us can withdraw and invest as he or she chooses. Many people are unable to properly manage these funds; those who can are far more likely to prosper.

There are countless success stories of American entrepreneurs who started on a shoestring and, over a period of time, became extremely wealthy. For instance, physicians and, in particular, surgeons, invest many years attending medical school, followed by years of internships and residencies—but later in their lives, they reap the rewards with their high earning power. Predictably, individuals with higher educations realize substantial lifetime earnings above those who do not attend college. Here, too, an investment in time and effort is made.

It's sad to see the high numbers of today's young people who are so anxious to acquire wealth but unwilling to pay the price that success demands. Instead, they seek shortcuts, which in the long run are dead ends in disguise. Over the years, I've witnessed many young college graduates going from job to job, too impatient to advance and, as a consequence, bouncing from one low entry position to another, never sticking around long enough to progress into management. Too many become disenchanted with the real world away from campus life. Some of them underestimated the competitiveness in industry. Still others simply fail to realize that a college diploma is not an automatic ticket to success but instead just a token to gain entry into the arena.

When I started UCC, my initial investment was $1,000. At the time, a large capitalization was not a prerequisite. Instead, I invested my time and toil. It was rare when I didn't put in a twelve-hour working day during UCC's first year. In 1971–1972, there were only six weekends, including holidays, when I didn't work. My entire staff joined me to work at the home office on Saturdays. It wasn't until 1977 that we cut back to a half day on Saturdays. Later, we went to a five-day work week from June through Labor Day, then resumed the 5½-day weekly schedule for the rest of the year. Eventually my management team convinced me that with a two-day weekend, our productivity would not decrease. The proof of the pudding was that both productivity and the bottom line continued to spiral, so our national headquarters has since remained closed on weekends.

Several years ago, a young insurance agent approached me for my advice. During our conversation, he talked about his love of sports and how he was active in a softball league, a bowling league, and, in addition, was an avid golfer. He also had two small children for whom he cared each evening while his wife worked her night job as a nurse.

He complained about how difficult the life insurance field was and how he struggled to make a living.

"I'm not making enough sales," he sighed.

"It doesn't surprise me," I replied. "There simply aren't enough hours in the day for you to participate in your other activities, care for your kids, and see enough prospects to generate the sales you want."

"What do you suggest I do?" he asked.

"You have a choice," I said, "but it depends on your priorities. You can either cut down on your ball playing and put in the proper effort to see enough prospects to close sales, or you can continue as you're doing and eventually be forced out of the insurance business."

"But I've played ball all my life," he said. "I like the business. It's only the lack of commissions I don't like."

"Since you asked me for advice," I continued, "I suggest you find some form of exercise program that occupies only forty-five minutes of your day. By the way, how many hours of sleep do you get each night?"

"Eight hours."

"Cut it down to seven hours, and once you adjust to less sleep, you'll do just fine. The forty-five minutes of morning exercise will be more beneficial to your general health than the extra hour of sleep," I advised. "And as far as your two young children are concerned, I appreciate your wanting to spend as much time with them as you can. At this point in your life, however, you must decide for yourself whether giving up some time with them now is worth being able to better provide for them and spend even more time with them in the not-too-distant future."

We then calculated how he could pick up an extra twelve hours a week to be spent with prospects. We also figured that his time, based on his present earnings and the actual hours he spent with prospects, was worth $50 an hour. "If your priority is to earn more money so you can provide your family with a better standard of living," I said, "I recommend you put in an extra three to four hours of evening calls several times a week. If you do, you'll have no more money problems."

At first, he seemed hesitant about spending so many hours away from his family. "Now, the way this will work," I continued, "is that for the next two years, you're going to have to put in twelve-hour days. However, by doing so, you will build a solid base of clients. This is the investment you must make in your business. Once you have the clientele, 80 percent of your new sales will be generated either from repeat business from these clients or from referrals they give you. Of course, you'll always have to prospect for new clients, but it will no longer require twelve-hour days because you'll have so much repeat business and referrals going for you.

"This is the price you must commit yourself to pay if you want to succeed in the life insurance business. If you aren't willing to make this investment of hard work and long hours, you may as well call it quits now, because you won't make it. What's so sad is that if you do quit, sooner or later you'll realize what I just laid out for you is applicable in every sales position. If this is asking too much, I advise you to get a desk job and resign yourself to a life of mediocrity."

The shine in his eyes was all I had to see. He got my message. He followed my advice, and within six months his earnings doubled. Today he is able to play golf three times a week and spend quality time with his children, and his wife quit her night job. He is also a member of his company's President's Club.

## Spending Money to Make Money

A growing business never has a shortage of places to put money. Whether it's spending money on new equipment, more office space, hiring additional people—the decision to spend money in order to make more money always prevails.

Decisions of this nature should be cut and dried. If it's good business, you do it. Pure and simple. It's as if you own a car that you are going to sell. It needs a paint job, some minor body work, and a major tune-up. Once you have done your homework and know what the going price is for comparable cars ranging from excellent to poor condition, you can determine whether the cost of the repairs will increase the value of your car in excess of what you would have realized had you sold it as is. Naturally, there is always a risk that you will spend more than the extra amount the buyer pays for the car, but by doing your homework, you should be able to make a valid decision on what to do. Certainly the same risk also exists in business, but this is the nature of the game.

When UCC was a small business, the decisions made to spend money, no matter how small an amount, were just as carefully thought out as decisions we make when spending large amounts today. In the early years, even putting in an additional telephone line or purchasing a new typewriter was issue for debate. I remember the old days when I shopped around to get the best price for some brochures, which at the time seemed like a big expense. We'd always be at the mercy of the printer and have to sweat it out, worrying whether our order would arrive in time. Eventually we invested in the development of our own printing department. Later, we added an audio department, which has since expanded into the production of audiovisual tapes. Our printing and audiovisual departments represent sizable investments to us, but the money spent for these departments represents a short-term sacrifice that will ultimately produce long-term gains.

The "sacrifice" involved in spending money is, of course, relative, depending upon how much money you have. While our investment in an audiovisual department was a major one for us, it would be small potatoes for a company such as Ford Motor Co. or IBM. I recently read that Ford has the world's most sophisticated satellite communications system of any nongovernment-owned enterprise, one that relays televised messages to its worldwide operations around the globe. It took only a ten-minute presentation to the appropriate executive committee, and the formation of Ford Communication Network (FCN) was unanimously approved. While Ford does not disclose the cost of FCN, it is estimated to run in the eight figures. As I said, everything is relative.

## Biting the Bullet

Sometimes a short-term sacrifice necessitates the termination of an operation due to a legal obligation or to protect one's reputation. A difficult decision of this nature is made with an eye toward the future, and requires both courage and belief in one's mission. It also requires an admission of error, which is particularly painful to a manager with a big ego.

The recalling of a car by an automaker is a good example. To recall a million cars is an expensive public disclosure that the company's product has a problem, but for legal and safety reasons, automobile manufacturers have no choice but to admit their error and invest in the solution. Under another scenario, the owner of a chain of retail stores might close several outlets that have been operating in the red. Even so, the rents must be paid for leases that could conceivably continue for periods running as long as twenty years or until a subtenant is secured. Or, as I discussed earlier, a major corporation might conclude that its multibillion-dollar acquisition has been a financial drain and decide to bite the bullet by selling it, thereby taking a substantial write-off.

Because UCC is a people business, the success of each individual club is predicated on the performance of its management. For an array of reasons, such as incompetent and/ or unscrupulous franchise owners, or still others who became wealthy and chose to retire, clubs have been closed. Obviously this presents a problem because it leaves members in a particular community without a club at which to use their membership. There is no legal obligation on the part of UCC to maintain a showroom in the area. Basically, it's no different than if a GM-franchised Cadillac dealership goes out of business. Under those circumstances, GM is not legally obligated to continue to operate a Cadillac service department to replace the defunct dealership.

Yet, even though UCC is not liable to the membership of a club that folds, we can ill afford to blemish our reputation. So, rather than allow our members to get hurt, we have many times elected to keep the showroom open to service its existing membership. Since our revenues come from the fees collected by the sale of new memberships and nominal renewal fees, semifunctioning clubs have large overheads, which generate substantial financial losses. They can only be turned around by reselling the franchise or by transferring somebody to the area to again operate it. Nonetheless, we continue to operate such clubs at a loss.

When our first club in Anderson, Indiana, was closed in 1974, its owner stuck us with an $80,000 debt to several furniture manufacturers. He had spent the money the members had paid in advance for orders and consequently did not have it to pay the manufacturers upon delivery. As a franchisee, he was an independent business owner, and he was liable, not us. But he was broke, and as the saying goes, you can't get blood out of a stone. In those days, $80,000 was a huge sum of money to us, yet we paid off every penny due the manufacturers and made sure every member received his or her merchandise. We then continued to operate the club, sustaining a heavy loss until the Anderson franchise could be provided with new management. How well we understood that our reputation was at stake. We knew that the demise of a single UCC franchise jeopardized the reputation of all our clubs. We refused to strand a single consumer who paid for a UCC membership.

While it was not the intention, our commitment to the members of those early clubs that failed later became a strong selling point. It has also showed every attorney general's office that we are an honorable organization.

Sure, we've had our failures along the way, and when we do, we pick up the pieces and do whatever is necessary to correct the situation. Every organization, as well as every successful individual, is bound to fail now and then. The only ones that never do are those who never take risks. And without some risk taking, long-term gains are limited.

## The Perils of Quarteritis

A major disease that many publicly owned American corporations suffer is "quarteritis," a sometimes fatal affliction in the business world. It's a sad state of affairs, but somewhere along the line, the American business community decided that scorecards of our public corporations' performances should be kept on a three-month basis. So every ninety days, quarterly financial reports are routinely published for review by anyone who so desires, including shareholders, Wall Street analysts, corporate raiders, competitors, and the merely curious.

On the other hand, in Japan the financial reports of publicly owned corporations are published only on an annual basis. They're not so anxious to release such information because their interests are oriented toward long-term thinking—with little concern about short-term results. Furthermore, their large shareholders are usually such allies as banks, insurance companies, and institutional investors who understand that by meddling in management and stressing short-term profitability or cost-cutting measures, they will cause long-term gains to suffer. It is no wonder that Japanese companies are more prone to pour money into research and development, even though it looks bad on the balance sheets. While American corporations are prone to slashing research and development expenditures when heavy losses are suffered, Japanese companies tend to increase them. Unlike American stockholders, Japanese bankers have less interest in realizing a temporary boost in corporate earnings with the corresponding rise in the market value of its traded stock than in continued focus on the company's long-term success. Their concern is geared toward making sure a corporation that borrows from them is healthy, pays the interest on its debts—and grows.

UCC is a privately owned corporation and, consequently, we are not required to file financial reports to be viewed by the public. We are in an enviable position whereby we have no need to raise capital by selling ownership in our company. Accordingly, we are not likely to be afflicted with quarteritis.

## Beyond Financial Rewards

Obviously profits are both desirable and necessary. No enterprise can have an ongoing flow of red ink and remain afloat forever. Yet even though managers need a strong profit motive, the objective to managing a business should never be purely to make money.

When I founded UCC, I did so to provide consumers with an alternative to buying retail. I was obsessed with a dream of establishing a coast-to-coast buyers' club that would have tremendous buying power and thereby enable its members to realize substantial savings by purchasing merchandise at manufacturer's cost. If I could realize this mission, I believed it would be a wonderful contribution to millions of people, who could, in turn, improve their standard of living.

My ambition was not to obtain wealth. When I hear people say that they are highly motivated by their ambition to be rich, I consider them either confused or consumed with greed. Plus, those whose only aim is to acquire wealth have no direction. However, with the realization of a clear, concrete goal to create something worthwhile and make a contribution to others, only then can great fortunes be amassed.

For the record, I'm all for financial security. I love my family and was driven to provide them with a high standard of living. I wanted one for myself, too. But most importantly, I always understood that if UCC was able to do the wonderful things that I had envisioned, affluence would automatically follow. Yes, my rewards came, but only when UCC was able to provide to others what it was originally established to provide.

I believe most achievers in this world think along this line. Imagine an individual who wanted to be a heart surgeon but only because he or she desired to be rich. Such a doctor is not one I would choose to perform my open-heart surgery! Neither would I ever buy an insurance policy from a salesperson who only saw dollar signs whenever he or she looked at me. Nor would I want such an architect to build my home. I did, however, hire an architect to design my recently built dream house, a man who was dedicated to creating what he and I believed would be a masterpiece that would be an immense source of pride to both of us. It is evident that the doers in this world want to leave their mark—they're not driven by what's in it for them.

Today, I have wealth that far exceeds what I have ever imagined. And I continue to build, not to create more wealth, but because I love my work, I love the people with whom I am associated, and it is my greatest joy to see them grow and prosper. I also love to see so many club members benefit from UCC's services. And when you find something you love to do, you'll never work another day in your life.

# —7—
# THE VITAL TRANSITION

WHEN I READ THE CHRONICLES OF America's colossal global corporations, I marvel at how many have come from humble beginnings. The H. J. Heinz Co. has roots that trace back to 1869, when its founder made and bottled his ketchup in the family kitchen. Ford Motor Co. began in a garage in 1903 with a cash investment of $28,000. Less than nine decades later, Ford became a $94 billion corporation. And IBM originally was the Computing-Tabulating-Recording Co., a small manufacturer of meat scales, when Thomas Watson, Sr., acquired it in 1914. Avon, Coca-Cola, and Sears also are notable examples. More recently such prestigious enterprises as McDonald's, Holiday Inn, MCI, and Apple Computer have made that remarkable transition.

Earlier I stated that it's hard for me to imagine anyone starting a business without having a desire to make it reach its fullest potential. I am, however, aware of the obstacles and disappointments that undermine the dreams of less determined men and women. I also have empathy for the fledgling entrepreneur, who, against great odds, struggles to launch a new venture. It is a rare phenomenon when a new venture enjoys a continuous climb to the pinnacle of success. It's a bumpy journey to the top, with the valleys more pronounced than the peaks.

Naturally, companies recognized on such lists as the Fortune 500 represent only a small fraction of the countless entities that have been founded in the United States. There are thousands of existing mom-and-pop operations and even more that have vanished.

This chapter is dedicated to those men and women who have survived the trying years and remain neither tainted nor disillusioned. They remain committed to fulfilling their ambitions and are dedicated enough to make the vital transition from a small enterprise to a large organization.

## A Tale of Two Different Talents

The building of a small company into a major corporation is rare. The businessperson capable of this is indeed an unusual individual, because what it takes to succeed as the founder of a small business is a far cry from what is necessary as an executive who manages a large corporation. The skills required are completely different. And without both sets of skills, free enterprise as we know it in America would cease to exist.

Even though I have an entrepreneurial background, I have the utmost respect for the men and women who are professional managers. It takes tremendous skill and motivation to begin a career at entry level and, within a corporate environment, work one's way to the top echelon of a large company. Achievement of this nature is considerably different than my life's work as an independent businessperson, and it is improbable that, had I chosen a corporate career path, I would have thrived in such an atmosphere.

Moreover, I have talked at great length to professional managers who expressed doubts that they would have fared well as entrepreneurs. The contrast is striking. Typically, a corporate recruit begins a training program, has managers to guide him or her, and, of course, is paid a salary. A well-managed corporation is structured to permit individuals on the fast track to advance on a timely schedule to positions of more responsibility. On the other hand, a founder of a business receives no training, nor does anybody manage that person. He or she is not paid a salary and, in addition, must put capital into the venture so as to someday realize a profit. Not only does the founder have no guarantee of being compensated for his or her efforts, a risk exists that his or her entire investment could be lost!

A classic example that illustrates the difference between entrepreneuring and corporate management is John De Lorean and his ill-fated attempt to launch his own automobile company. Prior to forming the DeLorean Motor Company, De Lorean was one of General Motors' rising stars. After having joined GM in 1956, he advanced to the position of general manager of the Chevrolet Motor Division in 1969 and was the youngest man ever to hold that position. By 1972 he was named group vice president in charge of all North American car and truck operations—which, by 1973, accounted for 87 percent of General Motors' profits. That year he resigned, and two years later De Lorean started his own company.

De Lorean was a superstar at GM, the world's largest industrial company. But operating his own business was a much different proposition. While his experience at GM provided him with the necessary know-how to arrange for the design, engineering, and construction of a car, he knew nothing about raising the millions of dollars required to finance his new business venture. As De Lorean has said,

> As an operating executive at GM, all I knew about financing was that if you needed $500 million to build a foundry somewhere, you'd fill out a form and send it off, and a few months later permission would come back with all these signatures saying, "Go ahead and spend $500 million." GM had an infinite amount of wealth. But that's not the way it works when you're one lone engineer trying to finance a car! With the particular combination of jobs I had in the automobile industry, I didn't know anybody in

the investment banking community or, for that matter, in any other industry. I knew absolutely nothing about raising money.

A small entrepreneur cannot be a specialist in only a single facet of his or her business. This person's job description is much more diversified and in the beginning is likely to include everything from obtaining financing to emptying the wastepaper baskets. The entrepreneur must fill a jack-of-all-trades role.

## As Your Business Grows, So Must You

The entrepreneur and the professional manager begin their careers much differently. When a highly successful entrepreneur's business evolves into a large corporation, however, his or her executive functions begin to more resemble those of the professional manager. In many ways, the entrepreneur and the corporate career person are like day and night. Yet, as a small business venture grows, its long-term success depends upon its founder's ability to make this transformation and to be able to assume a new role. A venture that began as a one-person operation is certain to be managed differently when it employs large numbers of people and does business on a vastly larger scale. Its management style must mature simultaneously, keeping step with company growth. A vital transition occurs, but generally so subtly it goes unnoticed by a casual observer.

It's probably a good thing this transition doesn't occur overnight. A gradual occurrence provides a business owner with some crucial time to adjust and grow into the position of operating a business on a higher level. In 1975, when John De Lorean started DeLorean Motor Company, the automobile industry was considerably different than when Henry Ford began his company. In 1903 alone, Ford Motor Co. was only one of fifty-seven new entries into the new American auto-making industry. In 1975 it was no longer possible to start a small automobile company. The last to succeed was Walter

Chrysler in 1924. De Lorean needed an estimated $200 million to finance his new venture. Had he been able to start on a small scale and gradually learn and grow with his company, the DeLorean Motor Company might have fared better. But such an opportunity no longer existed. In mature industries, large sums of venture capital are required.

When I first formed UCC, I sometimes wished I had a group of investors available to infuse a few million dollars into my new venture. Back then I felt that, with money behind me, the business could expand at a much faster pace. I envisioned United Consumers Clubs spreading like wildfire and rapidly becoming a household word in America. In retrospect, such an early expansion program would have been disastrous. As pioneers in our industry, we had to learn by trial and error. Had we made some of our earlier blunders on a grand scale, UCC would have been wiped out. We had to learn the business from the ground up. Furthermore, none of us had the managerial background to operate a large organization. As the business grew, we grew with it, and we eventually developed the necessary skills to be proficient in our present duties.

## The Art of Delegation

Delegating responsibilities does not come naturally to an entrepreneur. In the beginning, an individual who starts a business as the owner of a one-person operation has no choice but to do everything because, if he or she doesn't, it doesn't get done. After all, there is nobody to whom this person can delegate. Like a mother who nourishes and protects her infant, so does a small-business owner nourish and protect the venture during its infancy.

It is natural for such people to think they know their business better than anyone else. They do. It therefore often seems unnatural for them to relinquish authority and willingly share the decision-making role.

I don't believe that anyone is born a delegator. One is no more born to delegate than to practice law or medicine. It's

an acquired skill that's learned gradually and, most commonly, out of necessity. For example, there comes a time
when an individual who operates a small machine shop must
eventually stop unloading trucks, because performing such
menial chores limits his or her output. Unless the shop owner
can delegate repetitive tasks, his or her business cannot expand past the point of what the owner produces personally.
To grow, it's imperative to assign tedious chores to somebody
else.

In all probability, the owner will relinquish these duties
gradually. At first, he or she may hire a youngster to come in
after school to unload trucks. Only later might the owner hire
a full-time employee. He or she must be willing to teach a
part-time worker and, most importantly, believe the new
worker can do the job adequately. Although the entrepreneur
realizes that a helper might not do the job as well as he or she
did, it's still a move forward to become free for more important work. The owner next must train the worker how to stack
the goods as they come in and to keep a proper accounting of
each shipment. This requires trust that the new employee
won't steal from him or her. Without this trust, the owner is
not able to be productive in another area of the business,
because he or she is always keeping a watchful eye on the
employee. Assuming this employee's ability and honesty does,
indeed, fall within acceptable limits, the company's expansion
can begin. While the business owner strives to educate the
helper to be as conscientious and proficient as he or she, even
if the worker never achieves the same degree of proficiency,
the delegation still increases total productivity.

This is progress and what I refer to as my one-plus-one-
doesn't-equal-two theory. Simply put, my theory is that responsibility is given to somebody, and, although the second
person might not perform as well as the business owner, two
jobs are performed, and the total production exceeds the
output of a single person's efforts. Furthermore, the additional revenue generated will exceed the cost of the worker's
wages, so a profit is realized.

Suppose, for example, someone operates a successful one-
person doughnut shop. It demands the owner's full time and

efforts, and the small business is profitable. Its success inspires the owner to open a second shop, which requires a store manager. "This store will duplicate what I do at my first store," the man says, "and my income will therefore increase." But since the employee does not have a proprietary interest in the business, it is certain that he or she won't be as motivated as the owner. This does not mean, however, that the second store shouldn't be opened. At the onset, the owner should not expect the second store to do as well, unless some other factor exists, such as a better location or more modern equipment. Then, too, the original store might suffer a drop in sales, since it will receive less attention from the owner, who must also visit and supervise the second store. In spite of the two doughnut shops not making twice the profits of the first, with good management, the total revenues will exceed those of the single store. As still more doughnut shops are opened, the profit margins per unit are likely to be lower than the original store's, but as a result of the owner's ability to apply leverage, the total earnings will be greater. So you see, even when one plus one equals only one and a half, it represents a very worthwhile 50 percent increase in productivity.

Delegation is necessary for expansion. I realized this from the very start and devised my game plan to open UCC clubs across the country. If I had devoted my full efforts to a single club with no thought of expansion, I am certain it would have been bigger than any of our existing clubs. At best, however, it could only produce what two or three top clubs generate— a single club could never approach our present volume. If Ray Kroc had opened a single McDonald's restaurant, the same one-plus-one-doesn't-equal-two theory would be applicable. The world's largest single restaurant is minute in comparison to today's McDonald's with more than twelve thousand stores around the world.

## The "Home" Office

My first UCC employee, Armina Thorpe, began as a Manpower temporary secretary in 1967 when I was in the oil and gas business. She's still my secretary, and I don't know what

I'd do without her. I kept Armina on the payroll even when I was in between businesses, and the day I started UCC, working out of an office in my home, she was there by my side. My residence was UCC's "home" office for six months before we opened our first company-owned club in Shererville, Indiana, which also served as our national headquarters.

Like millions of other Americans who work out of their home, I did it to keep my overhead down. Not only was I able to avoid paying rent, I was able to get a nice tax write-off. I put in fourteen-hour days, weekends included, so working at home allowed me to spend some spare moments with my family. I particularly liked having an occasional lunch with them, and I enjoyed not having to fight the rush hour traffic to and from work.

Those are the advantages of working in a home office, but I'm convinced the disadvantages outweigh them. First, there are simply too many distractions in a home environment. Children, spouse, and pets are the most obvious. Then there's the temptation to turn on the television, take a nap, cut the grass, and so on. Still another drawback is other people's reactions. Many people don't take your business seriously, and they treat you as if your time is less valuable. When I worked out of my home, I was amazed at how many friends called me to play golf, go fishing, or take in a ball game. It was as if I was expected to always be available.

The main problem, though, is that a home isn't set up to have a business operating on its premises, so work also interferes with one's personal life. Either way, my advice is to get out of the house as soon as your budget can afford the move. If your goals are to expand beyond a one-person entrepreneurship, the sooner the business is situated outside the home, the better. While you may feel comfortable working in your home, employees probably do not. They feel like they're intruding on the privacy of other members of the household— and they generally are.

If you can't afford to make the move, it's imperative that you exert exceptional self-discipline, which is a difficult task for most people. For instance, a friend who was a successful real estate developer thought working in his huge 15,000-square-foot home would offer a comfortable lifestyle. However, he couldn't resist the temptation to raid the refrigerator. After gaining a quick twenty pounds, he decided that his home and office should indeed be separate. It didn't work out for another friend because he was *too* disciplined. He never stopped working! In the evenings, after watching a few minutes of television with his wife, he'd excuse himself to "check on something" in his office. Once he stepped into the office, he'd stay there until midnight.

In order to work efficiently in one's home, one needs the entire family to cooperate. I recommend establishing certain ironclad rules by which everyone must abide. For example, I announced to my wife, Claire, that during my office hours I was unavailable for grocery shopping, running errands, or carpooling. Nor did I baby-sit, feed dogs, or wait on repairmen. "Those weren't my responsibilities when I worked at my other office," I said, "and if I am to succeed in launching a new business, I can't be burdened with such chores just because my office now happens to be in our home." I was able to function in my home, but only because Claire gave her full support and cooperation. In general, most spouses get in the way, and it puts a strain on both the business and the marriage.

In a state of frustration, another friend laid down the law to his wife and said, "I need you to show the same respect for my time now as you did when I practiced law at an office in downtown Chicago. From now on, I don't want to be distracted by anything that goes on around the house. I don't care if the house is on fire. Don't tell me about it—call the fire department. I'll find out about it when I see the fire engines parked outside!"

## The Bigger the Business, the Bigger the Headaches

I'm all for people stretching themselves to reach their maximum potential. But you must never strive for bigness if it means compromising quality. It's usually quality that generates the original success. Once quality is lost, the business becomes void of its attraction to its customers.

A man may own a fine restaurant that seats only eighty people. He turns his tables twice a week on Fridays and Saturdays. To increase his revenue, he moves to a larger location that can handle two hundred-fifty customers per seating. Like many other restaurateurs who have made the same mistake, his business is no longer able to provide the same service and quality as when it was small. The personal touch that the owner gave his small restaurant is no longer possible. Due to increased turnover, the manager's interaction with the public must be delegated to others, who don't take the same pride in serving the customers. Additional cooks must be hired to do work that was previously his sole responsibility. Some specialized talents (in the case of a restaurateur, culinary skills) are simply not transferable. An entrepreneur cannot delegate to others what requires a unique ability that only he or she possesses. In this situation, doing business on a larger scale can have predictably disastrous results.

Big by itself is not always better, but for years Americans have been obsessed with it. "Big, not best, has always been the American calling card," Tom Peters wrote in *Thriving on Chaos*. "I bet you can't drive more than seventy-five miles in any direction, from anywhere in the United States, without running into a 'biggest in the world' of some sort."

The success of a business should not be measured merely by its size. Too often, fast-food restaurants and retail stores keep score based on how many outlets are opened each year. Even our leading law and accounting firms state their successes in numbers of partners, associates, and offices when making comparisons with their competition. Listen to a group of Fortune 500 CEOs talk after the annual rankings come out, and the most common question asked is, "What's your rank?" Making the Fortune 500, an achievement based on size alone, is the Holy Grail for most outsiders; moving up is the Holy Grail for most members.

It's important to remember that many headaches accompany operating a large company. Once you stop doing things yourself, the business requires more people, and with more people, there are more problems. In manufacturing, for example, management of larger companies must contend with unionization, and the demands made by union leaders present a collection of problems unlike any others. With a larger work force, there is also more turnover. And there is more paperwork, including group insurance, employee fringe benefits, and controls necessary to monitor employee theft.

In a 1986 survey by Robert Half International, a large recruiting consulting firm, it was estimated that American workers "steal" an average of four hours and twenty-nine minutes a week, which totals six weeks a year. In the study, the firm defined theft as the "deliberate and persistent abuse of job time." Examples of how employees cheat their employers include habitually arriving late or leaving early, pretending to be ill, using company property and time to take care of personal business, taking long lunch hours and coffee breaks, and creating the need for overtime by working slowly. Half said that about $197 billion worth of all United States employers' time each year is stolen. Small businesses get cheated too, but an owner who works beside his or her workers can personally police them. Additionally, due to their close relationship with the owner, employees are less likely to steal from him or her.

When UCC operated only in the state of Indiana, we only had to contend with Indiana law. Later, as we expanded into other areas, we had to comply with regulations that differ from state to state. Again, that meant even more paperwork. Of course, when an entrepreneur makes a public offering of the company to raise capital for expansion, considerable time and money must be invested in the additional paperwork resulting from securities regulatory agencies.

When UCC was a small business, we didn't make many waves; when our company became large, it attracted attention. When we were a small operation, retailers didn't consider us to be worthy competition. They didn't feel threatened. Later, when we grew and attained a higher profile, complaints increased to our suppliers that we were underselling them. We were accused of being unfair competition. About the same time, retailers began filing complaints about us to local and state agencies.

It's strange how things work. As a small entrepreneur, I thought there'd be fewer problems when we became bigger and stronger. Yet as we grew, I found that there was a whole new set of problems, and they were larger than I imagined. I suppose it never gets easy, but new and bigger challenges do make it more interesting.

## Money Doesn't Always Solve Problems— It Sometimes Creates Them

Nobody likes to run a business on a shoestring, but more often than not, a small entrepreneur has no alternative. Surveys indicate that the number one reason for failure of small companies is a lack of capitalization. Yet pouring money into an enterprise isn't necessarily a panacea for all problems. In fact, sometimes additional financial resources make absolutely no difference. For example, two hundred years ago, all the money in the world couldn't have put a man on the moon. Until certain technology was available, people lacked the capacity to fly an airplane, let alone launch a spaceship. Recognizing when increasing capitalization is appropriate is the key to fiscal responsibility.

When you have money, it's easy to throw some at a problem and think that money alone will be the solution. Instead, money sometimes aggravates the problem. This happens because you end up neglecting the real problem by trying to buy your way out of it. As a consequence, the problem still exists, but now it is ignored. For example, a business might expand to a point where it must replace a particular manager. When the company was small, this individual was capable of doing the job, but he failed to grow at the same pace as the business. Because it's always painful to discharge somebody, instead of replacing him, the prosperous company can hire an additional worker to do the job. The hiree reports to the incompetent manager, who feels threatened. A situation now exists where a person is subservient to a manager who doesn't want that person to succeed. In previous, less affluent times in the company's development, the owner would have been forced to deal with the problem more directly. Since the owner couldn't have afforded both employees, the new, more competent person would have replaced the manager. In a growing company that's cost-efficient, employees who don't maintain the same rate of personal growth fall by the wayside.

There are times when a small-business person who has enjoyed some brief prosperity foolishly invests his or her profits in unnecessary equipment. The owner of a doughnut shop might need another doughnut machine only once a month during a peak period when demand is high. While the purchase of a machine solves this occasional problem, its cost is so high that the extra sales don't warrant the additional expense. As a result, profits drop, even though more sales volume has been generated.

I've witnessed small entrepreneurs unwisely invest in equipment such as computers, car phones, and fax machines when the frequency of usage didn't support the costs. And it's a common occurrence to see "overnight successes" move out of originally modest headquarters into lavish offices and pay outlandish fees to interior decorators for elaborate furnishings. It's difficult for many entrepreneurs who can finally afford the trimmings of success to adjust to their newly found affluence.

## The Bigger the Business, the Easier Some Things Are

Some things, fortunately, do get easier when a business gets bigger. For starters, no more do I have to empty the trash cans, sweep the floor, or unload heavy packages. I've known individuals with Ph.D.s—people whose time was worth $200 an hour—who had to spend several hours a week doing chores that could have been performed by a minimum-wage worker. But that's the way it generally is when a business is too small to hire somebody. I vividly remember those days when I had to serve as my own part-time errand boy, janitor, and mailing clerk. I dreaded taking time away from my executive duties to do menial tasks. I felt it was an unproductive use of my time and physically draining. And it was frustrating to do the work myself when I knew that, as a business owner, my time was too valuable.

It didn't happen overnight, but today UCC is big enough to have full-time employees performing what used to be my odd jobs. I also have efficient staff people to do clerical and accounting work for me. My company operates on a large enough scale that these responsibilities can be delegated to others, and I can spend the majority of my time working in areas where I am more productive.

As a passive investor in real estate long ago, I learned not to shy away from large real estate ventures. There's little difference between the big deals and the little deals, because both have the same business principles. It's really easier to make a $20 million deal than a $200,000 deal. When a large office building or apartment building complex is purchased, it generates more income, and because it's done on a larger scale, better people can be hired to manage it. For example, a five hundred-unit apartment complex or a five hundred thousand-square-foot office building can afford to hire full-time maintenance people, have its own rental office, and so on. A small twenty-five-unit property or a ten thousand-square-foot office building can't operate on the same economies of scale. Its owner must collect the rent and personally deal with such headaches as leaking roofs and flooded toilets.

## Speed Bumps

Some people call them peaks and valleys. I call them speed bumps. Big, middle-sized, and small businesses alike have their fill of them. Only on rare occasions does an enterprise skyrocket without experiencing major setbacks along the way. The road is likely to be more rocky for start-up entrepreneurs because they must feel their way in the dark. Later, when they are more experienced and their business is more firmly established, things are more predictable, and foreseen hazards can be avoided.

UCC is now in its twentieth year, and for nineteen of those years, the company has operated in the black. But did we ever lose a bundle in 1977! That's the year we lost $681,000, a huge loss for a company capitalized with a mere $1,000 just six years before. We were seriously hurt, and we had to fall back. We now refer to that infamous day as Black Thursday; it's when I took decisive action that ultimately turned things around for the company. Looking back, it was a close call— so close, I feel blessed there is a UCC today.

I've since talked to a lot of successful entrepreneurs across the country and have heard similar horror stories about how they, too, nearly went under and considered quitting when their businesses looked so bleak. Nobody ever has a perfect record; we all make our share of mistakes. Plus, there are always factors beyond our control. No matter how smoothly everything seems to be going, there are those times when even the best of us hits a speed bump. When this happens, an entrepreneur must pay close attention to the business and figure out his or her problems. While some people like to sit on their problems, I like to act quickly and decisively; I won't allow anything to hang over my head. A speed bump is not the end of the road—it's just a minor obstacle.

## Records Are Made to Be Broken—Or Are They?

In America we've been ingrained with the desire to continually progress, that every year our performance should outdo the previous year's. Accordingly, managers are driven to produce more annual profits year after year. For a small business, it's no big deal to increase earnings by double- and triple-digit percentages during the early years. For example, jumping from $10,000 to $50,000 from year one to year two is a 500 percent increase—but note that it's only a $40,000 difference in one's bottom line. Later, when profits increase from $800,000 to $1,000,000, the increase is only 25 percent, but a $200,000 difference. As you can see, when profits are measured by percentages, they can be misleading. Even a decrease from $800,000 to $700,000 is better than an increase from $10,000 to $50,000. Which would you prefer your business to net?

On Wall Street, a main criterion that determines the market value of a company's stock is a comparison of its earnings from year to year. A "hot" stock is often one that has record earnings on an ongoing basis. If its profits increase by a lesser percentage, or are less than in the previous twelve-month period, in all likelihood the listed stock will lose favor with the investment community, and its price will tumble.

Even the most successful and best-run companies such as Coca-Cola, Ford, General Electric, and IBM don't rack up record earnings year after year. They shouldn't be expected to—no more than a star athlete is expected to jump higher or run faster every time he or she performs. Imagine the net worth that a company such as IBM would accumulate if its bottom line continually improved year after year. Consider the fact that IBM had back-to-back years with profits in excess of $5 billion in 1987 and 1988! When its net profit slipped to $3.7 billion in 1989, the company could hardly be considered failing because it didn't produce still more profits than the previous year. Yet, according to security analysts and the corresponding price decrease in market value of the company's stock, IBM management received bad grades. (The price of one IBM share reached a high of $175 in 1987 and dropped as low as $93 in 1989.) Likewise, companies in the fast-food industry have witnessed price decreases in their stock when the number of franchises opened in a twelve-month period tapered off. Here, too, if McDonald's continued at its record pace to open new restaurants, every corner in America eventually would have those golden arches.

Following Black Thursday, we stopped opening new franchises and concentrated our efforts on strengthening our existing clubs. This went on until 1981. The mere thought of what would have happened to the market value of our traded stock, had we been a publicly owned corporation, makes me shudder. We have since opened more franchises and now have announced the very real possibility of becoming multi-national.

While we continue to grow and refine ways of operating our business, we are aware of the possibility that more speed bumps will appear along the way. When they do, we'll know how to handle them.

# —8—

# YOU HAVE TO KISS A LOT OF FROGS BEFORE YOU KISS A PRINCE

IT'S NOT ONLY THE GAMBLING CASINOS that work the odds to give the house an edge. Every business has its own set of numbers. By definition of entrepreneurship, one assumes risks when he or she goes into business. The name of the game is to improve the odds for success. If we all had crystal balls, we wouldn't have to be concerned with the odds, because the future would be known. Instead, however, certain sets of ratios become valuable criteria for forecasting probable outcomes of important events.

In Las Vegas, projecting the casino odds is an exact science. The house's edge in such games as craps, roulette, blackjack, and keno can be found in dozens of published books on gambling. Calculating these odds is simply a matter of mathematics. Although it's not a mathematical certainty, when bets are placed on sports events, the odds makers book bets based, in part, on past performances of players and teams. Here, too, the bookmakers seek an edge. In business, there are too many variables to accurately forecast the future of a particular enterprise; in the case of a first-of-a-kind venture, the outcome is even less predictable.

142

UCC was one of those unpredictable ventures, because a history of a prior buyers' club didn't exist. For example, we couldn't forecast how consumers would react to our concept. Neither did we know if suppliers would permit us to sell their products. Nor could we accurately forecast what problems would arise. Even though I was able to put together financial projections to estimate revenues needed to cover expenses, I could only make "guesstimates." Like the first explorers who sailed in uncharted waters, we had no idea what was beyond the horizon.

Today, when a UCC club opens in a new city, we know what to expect. Based on its demographics and by making comparisons with other communities, we can forecast sales. And by knowing what expenses it takes to generate $x$ amount of revenue, we can also predetermine net profits. Today, many of the uncertainties I faced have been eliminated because we have an established pattern to follow. We know how to recruit the right people, and we can train them how to properly open a new club. Yet, because variables exist in people, we are unable to predict *which* individual will succeed. But what we can do is improve the odds by having franchisees do what experience tells us works best.

All successful franchisors operate on our proven modus operandi. We know that if a new franchisee does everything by the book, his or her success is highly probable. It's the individual who doesn't abide by the proven system who tends to fail. Studies have demonstrated that the failure rate of highly successful franchisors such as McDonald's and Pizza Hut is infinitely less than that of independently owned hamburger and pizza restaurants. Why do franchised operations have a much higher success rate? One major reason is that they operate with a developed, proven success formula—they *know* what works!

## The Law of Large Numbers

Years ago, I attended a sales meeting and learned a valuable lesson. The sales manager told the following story:

> BILL: How do you do it, Jake? How do you get all
> the women? You're not good-looking, and
> you're not all that smooth. What's your
> secret?
> JAKE: I just go up to every girl I see, and I say,
> "Hi, honey. How about a kiss?"
> BILL: That's it? Boy, you must get slapped a lot!
> JAKE: Yeah, and I also get kissed a lot!

The sales manager made his point. He went on to stress that the more calls a salesperson makes, the more sales will be closed. "You've got to play the numbers," he said. "If you see enough people, you'll get the sales." His pep talk reminded me about the fable of the princess and the frog. She had to kiss a lot of ugly frogs before she found her handsome Prince Charming.

I agree in principle with what the sales manager said, but he should have taken it further. A salesperson must deliver an effective presentation in order to make the numbers work to his or her advantage. No matter how many people the salesperson sees, the odds are overwhelmingly unfavorable if his or her presentation is weak. Had Jake taken more time to be better groomed and smoothed up his presentation, perhaps he wouldn't have been slapped so much.

Still, another analogy is a golfer who has never taken a lesson on his drive shot. This particular golfer's swing is so unorthodox and poor that no matter how many times he swings at the ball, it doesn't go anywhere. What's more, it's improbable that he'll ever have a 250-yard drive. Yet, with enough times at the tee, he might just get lucky and hit a long drive. As the expression goes, even a blind pig will stumble across some corn.

Given enough exposure, the law of large numbers always works with precision. For example, if a coin is flipped in the air ten thousand times, it will come within a fraction of one percent of having heads and tails each coming up 50 percent of the time. But if the coin is tossed in the air only five times, it's possible that one side may not appear. Furthermore, no matter how many consecutive times heads or tails appears, the odds are always even on each flip of the coin. With small numbers, the law of averages doesn't always work, but with large numbers, it's a certainty.

Life insurance actuaries determine the premium rates, for instance, on 100,000 lives at a specific age. At age thirty, actuarial tables project the life expectancy of a nonsmoking male to age seventy-four. This means that the total years lived by the entire group is 740,000 years, or seventy-four years per man. Naturally, it is likely that some will die before reaching age thirty-one, others before age thirty-two, and so on; likewise, others will live beyond age seventy-four. A life insurance company spreads its risk by underwriting large numbers of policies; if not, adverse selection can occur and result in more losses than what is predicted by actuarial charts. What every insurance company knows is that it cannot predict how long a certain individual will live. It can only accurately forecast the life expectancy of a large group of individuals. Then by spreading its exposure over many risks, it takes on almost no risk at all. The law of large numbers is the premise upon which the entire insurance industry is based.

A life insurance company's sales force also relies on the law of large numbers. If $x$ amount of agents give a sales presentation to $y$ amount of prospects, $z$ amount of prospects will buy. In the insurance field, there are more than two thousand life insurance companies selling products that, on the surface, seem much the same to the average consumer. With so many agents soliciting for the same business, prospecting for new clients is a major hurdle for every novice agent.

On a recent evening, I was reminded how crucial this is in the insurance field when I received a telephone call and found myself engaged in a brief conversation with a computer. Out of curiosity, following several beeps, I responded to such comments as, "Say 'yes' if you are interested in accumulating tax-free income for your retirement." "What is your present age?" and, "What is your current income?" Several days later, I mentioned this call to my agent. He explained that the machine automatically dials, talks, and records conversations with as many as five hundred prospects a day. "It's strictly a numbers game. Agents are satisfied to obtain one lead in one thousand calls if one out of three in-person presentations result in a signed application. These numbers make it profitable for the agent to use such a device," he explained. "But what about the poor 999 people who are interrupted during their supper by such impersonal calls?" I grumbled.

Generally, I'm cordial to telephone solicitors, because I know the majority of them are hardworking people trying to earn a living. Plus, I know what our salespeople are up against when they make cold calls. While we wouldn't consider using a machine, our salespeople, too, must make many calls in order to catch enough people in. Right from the start, they are taught to believe in the law of averages. They know that a certain percentage of people won't be home, another percentage will be available but won't be interested in engaging in a telephone conversation, and finally, there are those who will be receptive to receiving some literature about UCC. Several days later, a follow-up call is made to see if the literature was read, and at this time, the director invites these prospects to be guests at an open house. Approximately two out of the six people invited to a tour will actually show up, and 50 percent of those who attend will become members. Our salespeople are trained to understand how these numbers work—there will be days when nobody is home, and on other days, everything falls into place.

In the short run, the numbers can work for and against a salesperson, but in the long run, they always seem to average out. Luck has little to do with how well salespeople fare over a long period of time. Everybody gets his or her share of good and bad calls. But top salespeople consistently outproduce mediocre salespeople.

When a director or a club's production is down, we take a close look at the numbers. The numbers are very revealing; it's right there in black and white. A good thing about our system is that it's easy for somebody who's off track to be guided back on track. This is what I like so much about working with numbers. They always work.

## You Never Know *Which* Frog to Kiss

It would be a lot easier if the prince could identify himself so the princess wouldn't have to kiss so many frogs to find him. As a salesperson, you cannot tell in advance which prospects will be interested in your product. If you could, there wouldn't be any sense in calling the ones who weren't.

Vince Lombardi, the late football coach of the Green Bay Packers, used to say that out of the approximately 160 plays in a football game, 4 key plays determine which team wins. He insisted that his players exert their best effort on every play because there was no way to know which would be one of those four key plays.

Salespeople should never prequalify their prospects and think, "Oh, this person will never buy." It's wrong to judge somebody's interest in your product by appearances. It's wrong because appearances can be misleading. Believe me, I wish there was a way to know, before the fact, who would buy and who would not. A lot of extra effort would be saved. When $x$ amount of guests attend a UCC open house, we know that 50 percent of them will join the club. But we can't predetermine *who* will become a member, so our best effort is given to everybody.

## Raiding the Whorehouse

> "When they raid the whorehouse, they take the good girls with the bad girls."

I attribute this quote to a Wall Street broker in reference to a down market. Any active investor in the stock market knows that a major downswing in the stock market causes the market value of all companies' stock to decline—the good with the bad. In short, the overall poor performance of the market is likely to adversely affect stock prices of companies that, individually, should perform well.

Likewise, a fine retailer may take a bath as a result of having a lease in a poorly managed shopping mall. And a mom-and-pop bookstore might do a landslide business until three national franchisors set up shop in the same area. There are many external factors over which a businessperson may have little or no control—and some are completely unpredictable conditions that can have devastating consequences. An obvious one is the poor business conditions that arise as a result of severe economic conditions. A layoff of a large number of workers in a community can wreck business for the local establishments. When there's a national recession, there is a rippling effect, and the repercussions are widespread. Only a few scattered communities are left intact; the rest of the country gets hit hard.

Then there are times when pockets in the economy are weak while the nation as a whole prospers. In the early 1980s, for instance, the domestic automobile industry went through what it since refers to as the "automobile depression." As a consequence of the 1978 oil embargo, the Big Three's gas-guzzling behemoths were not able to compete with the more fuel-efficient imports, most notably the small, high-quality, Japanese-made cars. Hit hardest was Chrysler; only by being bailed out by the federal government did the company survive. And Ford, which lost $3.3 billion in 1980–1982, also was on its knees. Likewise, thousands of car dealers were forced into bankruptcy or simply shut their doors and took early retirement. Still later, in 1990, after Detroit had staged a comeback with record profits toward the end of the eighties, worldwide overproduction caused an automobile glut that again severely wounded the American car industry. Once more, car dealers across the country became victims of hard times.

When times get tough—on occasion as a result of circumstances beyond the control of an individual businessperson—the strongest of the fittest will survive; but it requires an intensified effort, and even then well-managed companies can go belly-up. By the nature of UCC's business, during prosperous periods, we enjoy the good times, and during recessionary periods, we also do well because people are then prone to look for better values. Yet, like all businesses, we are vulnerable to harmful external conditions. In certain areas, UCC clubs have been hurt because a fraudulent competing buyers' club misrepresented itself to consumers in a community. Through "guilt by association," bad publicity about these other buyers' clubs has made the public leery about joining any club—ours included. Such occurrences happen, and when they do, we must learn to live with them. The winners in this world learn to take the bad with the good.

## The Rejection Factor

In time, I suppose almost every salesperson develops an effective presentation and becomes proficient at selling his or her wares. In my opinion, few failures are due to a lack of ability to close sales; instead, salespeople fall short because they can't cope with rejection. I'm sure it's the number one reason for the high turnover in the sales profession. The ones who quit can't take the word *no*; they become discouraged and seek employment in nonselling jobs. For the record, I have never met anyone who likes rejection. I loathe it. But success in the sales field goes hand in hand with one's tolerance for handling rejection in a manner that's not self-destructive.

When I started UCC, I got it from both ends. Not only was I rejected as a salesperson when I sold memberships and franchises, I was constantly being told "no" by sales reps who refused to sell to me. I'll wager that I hold the record for being thrown out by more manufacturers at the mart than any other person in its entire history. If I had taken it personally, I would have quit. Whenever I was asked to leave a showroom, I'd say, "Maybe I didn't explain what we do clearly. Because if you understood what we're about, you'd be wining and dining me for our business."

"I heard you correctly. And I still don't want to do business with you."

I wasn't bashful about calling on the same people who rejected me the first time around. They'd see me coming and say, "Look, I've got too many people to see to stand here and hear your spiel again. Send me some literature or something." Or they'd simply say, "This is the third time you've been here, and I'm not interested. So leave, will you?"

I kept plugging away. I *knew* I had something that was exceptional, and I wasn't going to allow someone who didn't understand it to stop me. I knew that with enough calls, there'd be manufacturers who would see things my way. With the hundreds of manufacturers at the mart, it was just a matter of seeing enough of them before I'd find my share who would take UCC on as an account.

Once again, it's a numbers game, and I worked the numbers. All salespeople worth their salt understand that if they make enough *good* presentations, the sales will come. As I look back, it's somewhat embarrassing to be a *buyer* and get thrown out, but I applied the same principle in my efforts to convince manufacturers that they should sell to me.

When you do get a no, it should never be taken as personal rejection. Your skin must be thick. You can't allow your feelings to be hurt when somebody doesn't want your product. When a prospect doesn't buy, he or she is not rejecting you. The prospect just doesn't feel the need for your product. Or perhaps he or she can't afford it. And then it may be that there is something the prospect doesn't understand. Or perhaps you inadvertently failed to cover a pertinent point. Whatever the reason, it's not *you* who's the problem. How can it be? The prospect has no reason to dislike you.

And even if the prospect doesn't like you, so what? That's not the worst thing in the world. Not everybody is going to like you. That's a fact of life that each of us must accept.

## The Odds of Back-to-Back SOBs

If you call on enough prospects, you're bound to run into an SOB who will give you a rough time. There are simply too many of them out there; you can't avoid them. Every so often, you'll come face-to-face with somebody who has decided to shoot the next salesperson who walks in his or her office, and the last salesperson just left. When you meet with such an individual, you have to understand that it's just your turn. There's no reason for it. Some people are just plain mean. Or perhaps your timing is bad, and you've caught the prospect in an unbelievably rotten mood. Maybe his wife served him with divorce papers that morning. Maybe he just got chewed out by his boss. It could be that his biggest account canceled an order. Or perhaps his accountant just notified him that he owes a bundle in back taxes. Again, it's those numbers. In the long run they work for you, but in the short run they can burn you.

So what do you do when you get shot out of the saddle? The best thing is to write it off to the law of large numbers and recognize it as a part of selling. Nobody enjoys getting shot down, but it happens. The worst thing to do is to brood about it. An SOB who affects you like that has defeated you, and that was his or her intention. Don't let such a person beat you. Instead, be strong and go immediately to your next call. The odds against two SOBs in a row are incredibly high. Make a sale, and you can go home a winner.

## Being Abused Is Not Part of Your Job Description

There are some bullies in this world who just like to push other people around. Salespeople are their prime targets. These insolents think they can abuse a salesperson and get away with it, but they're wrong. Unless, of course, a salesperson lets them.

Always remember that there are worse fates in this world than losing a sale or an account (such as losing your self-respect). You don't have to take such abuse, and you shouldn't. Each time you permit yourself to be browbeaten, you lose a little of your self-esteem. Bit by bit, your self-confidence is whittled away. Never forget that your job is to sell and service customers, and you're engaged in making an honest living to support yourself and your family.

Customers have a right to disagree with you, but they don't have the right to shout at you or make derogatory remarks and get away with it. I've had prospects fly off the handle during a sales presentation, and I've said, "I respect your right not to buy, but I walked in here as a businessperson and a gentleman, and I resent your behavior." They're generally thrown back by such a remark. They expect a salesperson to walk out like a whipped dog or engage in a shouting match with them, but I refuse to bring myself down to their level. If I remain calm, they usually feel ashamed and apologize. If not, I walk out. I don't need their business, and I don't want it.

## When You're on a Roll, Don't Pass the Dice

Many salespeople have told me about how they sell in streaks. "I don't understand why it happens, but sometimes every-thing seems to fall into place. Everyone I call on is a 'perfect' prospect. It's as if I can't sell them fast enough. Then I have those days when I can't even give it away." Of course there are good streaks and bad streaks. Every salesperson has had one of those days when every call is a bummer. The prospect is out of town, is tied up in a business meeting, has had a bad experience with a salesperson from your company, is not interested in talking to any salesperson, and so on.

It works both ways. The numbers sometimes work out so some prospects appear as though they're waiting there for you with their checks already written. Part of the explanation for cold and hot streaks must be chalked up to mental attitude. When you're down, it's written all over your face, and you're sending a negative message to every prospect you see or talk to on the telephone (because it's in your voice, too). And when you're up, that also comes through. After you make a sale, your adrenaline starts to flow. Your spirits are high, and it carries over to your next call. You're more confident, and when you walk into a prospect's office with this attitude, it's a wonderful, contagious feeling. It's no wonder you get a good reception.

When you're in a slump, my advice is that you must stop and regroup. Give yourself a pep talk. Think about all of the satisfied customers you've sold in the past and now serve. I recommend that you stop by to visit some of your best customers; they'll reinforce your belief in the service and value they derive from your product. And while you're there, ask them for some referrals. And if they ask, level with them and say that you could use some leads. You'll be surprised at their willingness to help you.

Now back to those good days. When you're on a roll, keep the momentum going. Take advantage of your hot streak, and make some extra calls. Go for a record day!

# —9—

# GIVE YOURSELF AN EDGE

FOR THE RECORD, I don't advocate taking unfair advantage
of anyone. I also oppose the use of tactics that employ manip-
ulation. However, it is imperative that, whenever you can, you
seek to make things work for you rather than against you in
competitive situations. Preparation for a business meeting is
certainly ethical and aboveboard—your competitors have the
same opportunity to do their homework. While being smarter
than the competition does indeed provide an advantage, it's a
fair one; when you outsmart and outwork your competition,
you're probably going to outperform them as well.

Of course, in the majority of instances, you won't encounter adversaries in business, nor should they be viewed as foes.
For example, a seller and a buyer should be members of the
same team. Unlike a competitive event, after a successful
transaction occurs the customer and the salesperson both
walk away winners. The better a salesperson prepares and the
more effectively he or she delivers a presentation, the more
benefit the salesperson provides to the customer. It's a win-
win situation.

## Doing Your Homework

In today's highly competitive society, you have to do your homework. If you think you can slide by without being properly prepared, you're flirting with failure. I've seen a lot of businesspeople who opted to take the easy route. They weren't willing to acquire expertise in their field—after all, working to bone up on what is going on in the industry is a lot of extra work. Yet these individuals are the first to sing the blues when economic conditions go sour. And they refuse to take the blame for their failure; they simply tag themselves as victims of bad times. I call them volunteers in line for bankruptcy.

Unless your field is comparable to brain surgery or nuclear science, you don't have to be a genius to be successful. But in today's competitive world, it's essential to be an expert at your own business. In sales, it's considerably more difficult now than in the old days, when it only took a slap on the back, a few off-color jokes, and a round of drinks to get an order. The customer is too smart, and the competition is too tough in today's market for you to approach a prospect without doing your homework so you can make an intelligent presentation of your product. I don't care what you sell—you *must* make sure you know your business thoroughly.

A novice salesperson cannot accomplish this overnight. It takes time. This means that you must become a student of your industry. You must set aside the time to spend a few hours several nights a week studying literature about your market, your products, and your competition. Your objective should be to know everything there is to know about your business. Of course, it's unlikely that you ever will, so with this objective, your must enroll yourself in a lifetime self-improvement program. Strive for continuous improvement in every facet of your work, just as you would expect a heart surgeon or a tax attorney to devote long hours of his or her hectic schedule keeping up with the changes occurring in that person's field.

In addition to your home studying program, you should

attend seminars and seek out leading people in your field for advice. Enlist them as your mentors. They'll be flattered that you came to them, and it will be surprisingly easy to pick their brains. Furthermore, you should subscribe to publications that contain current changes in your industry. Of course, this advice is not limited to salespeople. It applies to everyone with a desire to succeed.

Being fully prepared means more than knowing your business backward and forward. It means anticipating events prior to entering a negotiation or meeting so that there are never any surprises. Over the years, I've attended many business meetings where knowledgeable managers failed to anticipate. As a consequence, their presence added nothing to the discussion, and their lack of preparation served as a hindrance to the meeting. In my opinion, there's nothing more presumptuous than somebody going into a meeting without being able to contribute to the others who are present. When such a person has to ask basic questions, it wastes the time of those who have prepared. Such behavior is downright insulting. That person is telling you, "I didn't want to be bothered with preparing because I knew everyone else would do it for me. So, let's take the time now for me to find out what I need to know."

The same applies to any salesperson who approaches me without the slightest idea about what UCC does. Due to the unusual nature of our business, I don't see how a sales presentation can be effective without some advance knowledge of what we do or, of course, what any business does. Yet I'm bombarded with calls by unprepared salespeople. I don't believe there are any circumstances that warrant this sort of unprofessionalism. It only takes a few calls in advance to find out something about us—a call to a nearby business, or to a salesperson who represents a noncompeting company, a visit to the local chamber of commerce, and so on. But for a salesperson to come in cold is inexcusable. While I'm receptive to salespeople, I come down rather hard on anyone who is too lazy to check us out before marching in here.

A salesperson should learn as much as possible about the nature of the prospect's business so unnecessary time isn't wasted asking basic questions. After all, it's not the customer's job to provide an education about the business so the salesperson can sell him or her.

Several years ago, Indiana's great basketball coach Bobby Knight addressed our Breakfast of Champions meeting, a seminar attended by our sales leaders. Knight delivered a powerful speech about how his team's national championship that season was directly attributable to preparation. In essence, his message stated that basketball games are won *before* the team steps onto the playing floor. He elaborated on how a championship team wins games by being in superior physical condition and wearing down the competition in the later minutes of a crucial contest. Knight also pointed out that tedious practice is required beforehand to develop precise teamwork. And he emphasized how his players were drilled on the strengths and weaknesses of each opposing player. In short, he made it clear that national championship teams don't simply show up at game time. "It's what we do *before the game* that wins the game," Knight insisted.

## Knowing the Competition

Like most top coaches in every sport, Bobby Knight studies films of his competition before a game. Champion boxers and tennis players also routinely focus in on their opponent's strengths and weaknesses before entering the ring or stepping onto the court. And leading baseball pitchers study the batting stances and swings of their league's hitters. The twenty-games-a-season winners know in advance what pitches are the most effective to throw at every opposing hitter.

In a sales presentation, a computer salesperson is at a disadvantage if he or she doesn't know what the competition has to offer. When a prospect says, "I want to shop around to see what ABC and XYZ companies are like in comparison to your model," a knowledgeable salesperson doesn't let this rebuttal stop him or her. The salesperson knows exactly what ABC and XYZ companies provide, and by demonstrating that his or her product, feature by feature, has them beat, can close the sale without allowing the prospect to cool off or, even worse, to be sold by the competition. It's not enough to know your product completely. You must know your competition's products, too.

Fortunately, you don't have to be a CIA agent to find out about the competition. For starters, read the trade magazines and the other guy's brochures that provide detailed product descriptions. There are a host of ways to obtain these brochures: you can write for them, request them by calling toll-free numbers, and ask your existing accounts to save all literature they receive in the mail and from sales reps. If you're in the retail business, you can "shop" your competition by routinely visiting their stores. In all likelihood, they're already shopping you, so don't be bashful about doing the same. If you sell Lincolns, for example, don't be shy about visiting the Mercedes and Cadillac showrooms. The chances are that the Cadillac and Mercedes salespeople have already visited yours.

In my business, we encourage our franchisees, managers, and directors to shop around at local retailers about once a month to see what they offer. In addition to developing their understanding about the competition, it's a tremendous morale-builder because our people sometimes forget how much UCC members actually save. Because our salespeople rarely buy retail, it's good for them to have some exposure to the treatment that retail customers receive when they shop. I like our salespeople to experience firsthand how most sales clerks fail to properly serve customers. In fact, it seems to take forever to even find somebody to wait on you in a department store these days, and when you finally do, the sales clerk acts as if he or she is doing you a favor by taking the time to talk to you. And lest our people forget, I want them to be reminded about how much more retail prices are compared to the values we provide our members.

## A Winning Attitude

Shopping the competition reinforces our people's belief in UCC, which, in turn, does wonders for their self-confidence. It's a terrific feeling for a salesperson to know without reservation that his or her product represents an outstanding value to the customer. Frankly, I can't comprehend selling something without believing in the product. When the conviction isn't there, the prospect is bound to sense it, placing the seller at a severe disadvantage.

I don't care what you sell, you must approach every prospect with the belief that he or she is going to buy. This belief must come from within, because you must first believe in yourself if you want others to. Novice salespeople ask, "How do I develop this self-belief? If I were successful, *then* it would be easy to believe in myself." In my book, the self-confidence comes first—without it, it's unlikely you'll ever succeed.

So how do you develop it? I believe it comes gradually. Once more, it's a matter of doing your homework so well that any time a prospect throws a curve at you, you know exactly how to handle it. But it takes time to become an expert in your field; you need a combination of study and experience.

You must also be convinced that your product is so exceptional that every buyer will receive a substantial value. And you must be confident in your company. Knowing that it's 100 percent behind you and the product is mandatory. Because no matter how much you believe in yourself and the product, if your company doesn't support your efforts and follow up by servicing your customers, you'll never realize long-term customer satisfaction. And if you don't, getting the initial order isn't, by itself, much of an accomplishment.

The salespeople who make it big are the ones who believe in themselves, their product, and their company. It takes all three to succeed—two out of three isn't good enough. These salespeople are easy to spot. They radiate self-confidence. It shows in the manner in which they walk into a prospect's office. It's reflected in their voice—during an in-person call as well as over the telephone. These dynamic individuals are able to get through to people who otherwise resist salespeople. And they're able to close sales with prospects who normally procrastinate when asked to make buying decisions. Winning attitudes are contagious, and once you have one, you'll want to make sure it's spread around.

## Presenting a Winning Image

There are two schools of thought about the image you present. The first advocates that you should go about your normal business without concern for it; in time one will automatically evolve. The second recommends that you give a high priority to creating your image while continuing to work at your main objective. I believe in the second—the image you project is too important to take for granted.

Every billion-dollar corporation in the United States sets aside a budget for promoting its image. To accomplish this, corporations spend millions of dollars annually to employ public relations staffs and to pay fees to outside firms for consultation. These are highly successful American businesses, and if they think it's worthwhile to spend large sums to present a winning image, I've always believed that it must make good sense for me also to be concerned about how I present myself. Now, I am not suggesting that you hire a director of public relations or an outside firm to start to work on your image. I understand that start-up businesspeople, salespeople, and individuals working for large organizations are not about to do this. Nonetheless, I do recommend that you devote some time and effort to doing certain things to improve your image. Having the right image is simply another advantage; it's one more tool to help you achieve your long-term objective.

The one most obvious facet that you can quickly alter is your physical appearance. I am not suggesting drastic changes such as plastic surgery or hair transplants, but I do believe attention should be given to personal grooming—such things as the clothes and jewelry you wear, the application of cosmetics, and the manner in which your hair is styled. If you're a banker or attorney, for example, a conservative dress code and hairstyle are appropriate. Similarly, if you're a salesperson who calls on bankers and attorneys, the adage "when in Rome, do as the Romans do" is good advice.

With one's personal appearance, consideration should be given to the nature of your work and the customs in the area where you live. A Wall Street attorney, for instance, should consider a more conservative appearance than an attorney in Hollywood or Las Vegas who represents show business personalities. Likewise, a life insurance agent selling to ranchers in Montana should follow a different dress code than another who sells to college professors in Boston. I won't elaborate on how to dress for success but will instead refer you to the dozens of books already published on this subject. The point I want to make is that people do judge other people by the way they dress, comb their hair, wear makeup, and so on. For these reasons, I urge you to consider how your appearance will influence people.

Of course, there are those who argue that appearances are only superficial, and people should be judged on more substantial qualities. In a perfect world I would agree, but in this less than perfect world you are judged by things as they appear on the surface, so you must concern yourself with how you are viewed by others. This is not to suggest that I believe only in artificial appearances and have no regard for actual substance. I do know, however, that all the substance in the world won't help if you can't get your foot in the door.

Once you become aware of the impressions people have about you, you will realize that physical appearance is only one area in which to direct your concern. Having your office in the right location is another key factor. How it is furnished and decorated is equally important. You may question what difference location and decor make, but let me give you an example: You have just met with two lawyers who appear to have the same education. Each came across as equally intelligent, and each has quoted you the same fee. The first lawyer has a plush office in one of the city's most prestigious buildings. His walls contain fine art, and his receptionist is attractive, polished, and professional. The second lawyer has a rundown office located in a blighted neighborhood. His carpeting is worn thin, the walls feature cracks and chipped paint instead of artwork, and his secretary was too engrossed in the *National Enquirer* to give you the time of day. Whom would you select to be your attorney to represent you in a personal injury case? I don't know about you, but the mental gymnastics in my mind would tell me to go with the attorney who is obviously (meaning, of course, apparently) more successful.

I think most people would share my opinion and choose to do business with successful-looking people. While it might not be something people think about consciously, their subconscious minds say, "There must be a good reason why this person is successful and this person is not. Evidently, the successful one is the better of the two!" It's a logical conclusion to think that a successful person is good at what he or she does.

People form impressions from dozens of little things: how receptionists and secretaries answer the telephone, the stationery and brochures received in the mail, the cars people drive, the clubs they belong to, the restaurants where they take clients, and so forth. While each by itself is not crucial, the total package you present is certain to make a difference. For anyone who wants to have an edge, I recommend giving some serious thought to these images.

## The Home Court Advantage

In sports, the odds makers always spot some points to the home team. In basketball, for instance, playing on the home court can be worth as much as six points. I think a home court advantage also exists in business, yet not everyone is smart enough to cash in on it. As I mentioned earlier, when UCC was first in business, we didn't either. For six years, we made house calls to sell memberships. It wasn't until 1978 when we finally wised up and started selling on our home turf.

Bringing prospects into our showrooms was the most important single revision in our marketing plan to increase our sales volume. When we sold in the home, prospects could only imagine what a club's showroom was like. It's much easier to give a newcomer a tour of our facilities so he or she can *see* the tens of thousands of catalog pages we stock at each club than to describe our catalog library. Then, too, there were many suspicious prospects who even doubted a showroom really existed when they first heard about our unique concept while sitting at their kitchen table.

It doesn't matter what you sell—if the prospect comes to your place of business, it's to your advantage—and, in all likelihood, to his or hers, too. For starters, you're more likely to have a captive audience. When you sell in a prospect's home or office, you can't control interruptions. Employees and customers are likely to barge in, telephone calls may require attention, and emergencies may arise. At your place, you can screen out all interruptions and have the prospect's undivided attention. Speaking of keeping the customer's attention, in Las Vegas, the gambling casinos have no windows or clocks. Once their customers are placing their bets, the casinos don't even want them to be distracted by the time of day, lest they might want to call it a night—or, for that matter, a morning!

An in-house presentation also offers the convenience of enabling you to show your full product line, which, depending on what you sell, is an important consideration. In our case, it is not physically possible for a salesperson to carry all of our catalogs to a prospect's home. So, in the past, only a handful of catalog pages were shown. Since it was not possible to know which catalogs would be the most alluring to each prospect, I am certain many sales were consequently lost. By the same token, neither can an office-equipment or furniture salesperson carry in his or her full product line. Certainly, a spacious showroom filled with a variety of models is a more effective way to display a computer or a copying machine than showing photographs. Plus, an actual demonstration of how a product operates has more appeal than a verbal description.

I remember when years ago a Xerox representative visited

my office to demonstrate a copying machine. It was a back-breaking and time-consuming job for her to bring it into my building; fortunately, I was on the first floor. After spending another twenty minutes to set it up, she was finally able to make the first copy for me. "That's a fine copy," I told her, "but I need a machine with the capacity to operate at a high speed." The poor woman, frazzled and drained, threw her arms up in the air and had no choice but to work from a work sheet that gave a description of several other models in her company's inventory. Today, Xerox sales reps invite prospects to their showrooms, where a large selection of models are displayed.

I previously mentioned how difficult it was in the early years for UCC to sign up suppliers. We'd visit dozens of trade shows, buying everything from furniture to toys. We'd also hopscotch across the country, stopping at manufacturers' plants and showrooms. Even though we wore the buyer's hat, we had to sell them on allowing us to carry their lines. Today, my son Jack, who serves as our vice president of merchandising, is responsible for determining what products UCC sells. Whenever possible, Jack encourages manufacturers to visit our headquarters in Merrillville. "It's so much easier to explain our business when they can see our operation," Jack explains. "If I can convince a major supplier to fly in to Midway or O'Hare, I'll send our limousine to pick him up, bring him here, and give him a tour of our facility. We have a very impressive building, and once somebody sees the phones ringing, the computers humming, and the orders coming in, he gets excited about the business his company can do with us. Things are really buzzing around here, so it's something that's far better to see than to hear about."

In today's world, it's becoming more and more common for the patient, the client, and the customer to leave his or her premises to receive treatment and service. Rarely does a physician make a house call. Instead, the patient goes to the doctor's office, where the equipment and nurses are located. Likewise, it's routine for clients to visit an attorney's or a

CPA's office. Even the most successful life insurance agents are inviting prospects to their offices. Recently, I had such an invitation: "I want you to come to my offices, Jim, because I'll need to do some computer runs for you to make certain projections for your estate planning. Let's do it at eleven-thirty on Thursday morning, and you'll stay for lunch. I have a new chef, who will prepare the best meal in town."

The insurance agent's walls featured an array of awards, certificates, and honors he had received. He also had some impressive photographs of himself with some VIPs that included the governor, a U.S. Senator, and a group of his golf foursome, all movers and shakers in the area. I noted how he used his walls to serve as billboards to promote himself. They delivered a visual message that wouldn't have been conveyed during a sales call at my office. He made good use of his home court advantage.

## The Power of Negative Thinking

For the record, I have no qualms with Norman Vincent Peale's classic book, *The Power of Positive Thinking*. Its message is right on target, and I'm all for positive thinking. I believe, however, that there's a danger in being overly positive, of failing to have a backup plan in the event that things go wrong. Quite frankly, the guy who sees the world only through rose-colored glasses leaves himself wide open to get it right between the eyes. In this respect, there is an advantage to thinking of the negative and planning what to do if the unexpected happens. For instance, in the Old West guns were known to jam, so the thinking man's gunslinger played it safe and packed two six-shooters. Along the same line, ships have lifeboats, fighter pilots carry parachutes, and cars have air bags.

In business, only a fool fails to have a contingency plan. During the hot roller-skating craze in the early 1970s, a friend of mine built a chain of rinks in the Midwest. They were expensive structures, and he knew the fad might last only for a few years. If so, the last thing in the world he wanted was to be stuck with a single-purpose building. With this in mind, he constructed roller-skating rinks that could be converted into warehouses. Because he had a contingency plan, he averted what could have otherwise been a financial disaster when the craze finally ended.

I'm always amazed when I see otherwise intelligent and sophisticated businesspeople fail to have a contingency plan. In a 1986 leveraged buyout costing $3.74 billion, R. H. Macy & Co. went private. In 1990, following a disastrous Christmas shopping season, the large retailer's debt skyrocketed to $5.67 billion. Campeau Corp.'s 1988 takeover of Federated Department Stores had a similar fate in early 1990. In 1987, Greyhound Lines, Inc., the nation's biggest intercity bus company, was taken private by an investor group that paid $350 million and relied heavily on junk bonds for the purchase money. By 1990, the bus company filed for bankruptcy to seek protection from its creditors. In each case, these debt-financed takeovers, riddled with high interest payments, failed to leave enough margin for error and unexpected problems. With Macy and Federated it was a poor Christmas season, and with Greyhound it was a three-month drivers' strike. Highly leveraged deals can work out when everything runs smoothly, but when things go even slightly bad, the whole business can go sour.

Every seasoned salesperson worth his or her salt anticipates objections during a sales presentation. This anticipation does not negate having the positive attitude that the prospect will buy. However, experience dictates that, for a variety of reasons, not every presentation results in a sale. Yet, when objections are overcome, an apparently lost sale can still be closed.

Our salespeople use a prepared sales presentation. The presentation has been structured to anticipate certain objections and has built-in rebuttals. Still, during or after the presentation, if a prospect expresses objections, our salespeople are equipped to answer them. Likewise, a successful businessperson has a contingency plan when negotiating an important deal. A top trial attorney is always prepared to change his or her defense when the opposition injects new evidence. And a winning coach has the flexibility to change the initial game plan during halftime to adjust to the opposing team's strategy. In every field, a contingency plan is vital, especially in today's complicated and fiercely competitive business world.

# —10—

# DO THE RIGHT THING

I'LL SAY IT VERY SIMPLY: *Doing the right thing is the only way.*

It's a shame that I find it necessary to include a chapter on this subject, but judging from what's going on in today's business world, too many people are way out of line. They're not doing what they know in their heart of hearts is the right thing to do. As an eternal optimist, I think people are basically good, and they want to do what's right. Unfortunately, there are too many hypocrisies in today's society, giving people the wrong messages. From Watergate to Wall Street, the American public has been witness to the moral erosion of our nation's political and business leadership for nearly two decades. As the 1980s ended, takeover artists and corporate raiders were amassing immense fortunes by attaining short-term goals aimed only at acquiring huge personal wealth. These modern-day robber barons neither built nor contributed.

Certainly the corruption of leadership does not justify the decay of an individual's ethics. It is not justifiable to plead that "the system" makes one cheat and bend the rules. Statistics have revealed that a large majority of workers take property belonging to their employers. They steal by taking incidental office supplies, and they cheat by showing up late for work, doing personal errands on company time, leaving before quitting time, and faking sick leaves. I'm alarmed to see people who consider themselves honest and fair-minded exhibit such behavior. No amount of rationalization that they are underpaid or that "everybody else does it" makes it right. It is wrong. Nor are they justified in stealing from their companies because others may cheat on income tax, pad expense accounts, or rip off customers. Wrong is wrong.

Since this is a book about success, I feel compelled to express my thoughts on doing the right thing—because to do otherwise is not only morally wrong, but self-defeating. I don't deny that it's possible to profit by acts of pettiness in the short term, but it's just that—a short-term gain. Over the long run, it will catch up with you. Eventually, subordinates and co-workers won't trust you, customers will stop doing business with you, and nobody, absolutely nobody, will be loyal to you. So, not only is it a rotten way to live, it is bad business. We live in challenging times, and I believe the real challenge is to succeed in such a way that you always maintain your self-respect and the respect of others. As Mark Twain said, "Let us endeavor to live so that when we come to die, even the undertaker will be sorry."

## Right Is Right

It doesn't matter what field you're in—manufacturing, sales, medicine, law, securities—right is right. If you don't choose to do something the right way, your only other alternative is to do it the wrong way. It's either black or it is white; there are no gray areas.

At first blush these are strong words. Since childhood, we are taught that life is full of compromises. And I agree, except when it comes to issues of right and wrong. Someone may ask, "How do people know what is right?" My answer is, "Because they know. That's how." I can't imagine anyone with enough brains to own a business or hold down a decent job who can't tell the difference between right and wrong. People may choose to do the wrong thing because it's more convenient or because they think it will line their pocketbooks. But they *do* know it's wrong.

Sometimes it's difficult to do what's right because we've been conditioned—and even taught—to do things that, deep inside, we know are wrong. For instance, I have a retired acquaintance who was in an automobile accident while vacationing in Sarasota. The accident occurred when he changed lanes without looking in his rearview mirror, and he was hit from behind. The driver of the other car was a poor migrant worker who spoke broken English. Nobody was injured, but the damage to both automobiles was extensive. My friend knew he had caused the accident; however, when the police arrived at the scene of the accident, he denied being at fault by conveniently failing to mention changing lanes. My friend is an articulate man who was neatly dressed and drove a luxury car. The migrant farm worker wore a dirty T-shirt and torn jeans; his car was a junker. The other driver tried in vain to explain his side of the story; the state trooper cited him for driving too closely to the car in front of him.

When my friend told me about what happened, he said, "I felt sorry for the poor guy, but what could I do? I feel terrible because the other driver can't afford to pay for his repairs, let alone the cost of the ticket and his premium increase."

"What could you have done?" I exclaimed. "You could have told the truth."

He looked at me as if I were crazy. "You must be nuts, Jim. I have always been told by my lawyer and insurance agent never to admit I was at fault in an accident. *Nobody* ever admits that an automobile accident was his fault."

My friend is basically a decent person. However, for years he has been brainwashed to do the wrong thing. I mentioned this incident to several other people, and they, too, held his belief, based on what they had been taught by insurance agents and attorneys. "Let the cops decide who's wrong," one said. "You don't have to volunteer information that is tanta-mount to confessing your guilt."

In the event of an accident where two drivers and no other witnesses are available, however, who is at fault can usually only be determined by what the two parties say. Therefore, the withholding of material information by either party is misrepresentation because, in the absence of the full facts, the truth is not revealed. In my opinion, stating only part of the facts is a lie of omission. I am aware that many people think differently—they believe that to lie one must say an untruth; they believe that keeping one's mouth shut is not lying. I disagree.

To carry this thought over to business, suppose a used-car salesperson failed to mention to you that the transmission was bad or that the brakes were shot. He did, however, tell you that the car was driven by an old lady who never drove when it rained or snowed. He also pointed out that the car had brand-new tires and its body was in excellent condition. While everything the salesman said was true, it's what he *didn't* say that was a misrepresentation. I am sure you'd share my thinking when the transmission slipped and the brakes had to be replaced a few days after you paid for the car "as is."

Recently I read that Mobil Chemical Co. was sued by seven states charging the company falsely claimed its Hefty trash bags and grocery bags would decompose. While it was true that the bags did, in fact, decompose when exposed to sun, wind, and rain, when they were incinerated or disposed of in landfills, their degradability was no different than that of ordinary plastic bags. A Mobil spokesperson insisted that the bags' degradability in sunlight was fully substantiated by tests and claimed the company never said its products would be the answer to the nation's waste-disposal problem.

It's my opinion that the ordinary consumer who picks up a package of garbage bags with the word *degradable* printed on it is given the impression that he is doing his part by paying more for such bags to save the environment. In his rush through a supermarket, it's unlikely that he will take the time to ask the question, "Yeah, but what happens if this product is covered with earth in a landfill and isn't subjected to the natural elements of sun, wind, and rain? Will it then decompose?" In such an instance, is a manufacturer guilty of withholding material information by knowing it is probable that the buyer will assume something different than what is actually stated?

There's a long list of instances of misleading advertising. I get particularly riled when false and blatantly exaggerated claims are made by food companies. Recently a parade of food manufacturers have promoted their products by adding the word *light* to the packaging. It is true that the word has a healthy and dietetic-sounding quality. Accordingly, a diet-conscious consumer interprets the message on a bottle of olive oil, for instance, to mean its contents have fewer calories or less fat, when, in fact, the product may only be lighter in color or in taste than competing products. Sara Lee Corp. claimed it was not trying to mislead people with its Light Classics desserts, which were subsequently renamed by the company to avoid a legal fight with a group of state attorneys general. A company spokesperson said its "light" was a reference to the airy texture of the products, not to their caloric content.

With the concern over high cholesterol in the United States, everything from cookies to potato chips now feature labels stamped "no cholesterol." This is true, but some of these items, by definition, have never contained cholesterol, because they are all-vegetable products. The manufacturers aren't providing products with a new benefit—but they're betting that you think they are. Obviously, many manufacturers are cashing in on the lack of knowledge of a frightened public.

I don't care what product or service you sell, it must be sold on its true merits, not by implication or inference. Even when a salesperson gives a totally honest presentation, and the customer is under the opinion that a specific feature is better than it really is, ethics demand that we give him or her a full explanation so there can be no misunderstandings. I don't buy the line, "Well, I told him, and it's not my fault if he didn't understand." That's bull! Of course it's the fault of the salesperson, and it is his or her obligation to reexplain the benefits to make absolutely sure the buyer knows exactly what he or she is getting—even if it means losing the sale. As I previously stated, it is not always what is said but what the buyer is led to believe that counts.

## The Right Thing for the Wrong Reason Is *Still* Wrong

Just as right is right, wrong is wrong, no matter what the reason. If a man, for instance, embezzles $100,000 from his company and gives the money to charity, he is still guilty of a wrongful act. Likewise, if I hire a minority woman for a technical position for which she has no qualifications, only because I want to give her employment, she is probably going to fail. Even though my act is based on a good intention, it will result in a bad outcome.

It's sometimes difficult to avoid doing a good deed for the wrong reason. There is a temptation to help others. It takes strength to say no, knowing that it hurts the other person, but, in truth, it is in his or her best interest. For instance, shortly after it was announced that this book was bought by a publisher, a woman who had been recently widowed sent me a handwritten, ten-page proposal for a manuscript. She wanted to write about the pain she and her deceased husband had suffered for several months before his death. A few days later, she called to discuss her book idea with me.

"I want to write a book about how my husband dealt with cancer," she explained.

"Why do you want to write it?" I asked.

"He was a wonderful husband and father, and it's a shame that he died so young," she said. "And I miss him so much."

After a lengthy conversation, I told her, "I am sure that Bill must have been a fine family man, and his death is a terrible loss to you and your children. Sadly, with the millions of people who die every year, a book about dying is not normally a subject that other people will want to read. Besides, there have already been so many books written about it. Now, if you want to write a book because by doing so, *you* will feel better—and it will be good therapy for you—then that's another story. By all means do it, and I am certain it will provide you with a deep sense of accomplishment. And if there's anything I can do to help you, please don't hesitate to call me."

We talked for a few minutes more, and I could tell she was in good spirits when we said good-bye. While it would have been nice to encourage her to write her book, I didn't think from the sampling sent to me that she was even close to having the writing skills to become a published author. Additionally, the chances of even a beautifully written manuscript being published about her husband's death were slim. The easy thing would have been to tell this grieving widow that her book was a great idea and she was sure to get it published. If I had done so, she would have been full of hope—but it would have been false hope. I also knew that it would be a far greater disappointment for her to spend many months of hard work writing it, only for it to be rejected by publishers.

## A Good Deal Must Be Good for All Parties

I've witnessed hard-nosed businesspeople walk away from the table grinning ear to ear and boasting, "I got him to sell me 100 gross of units at such a low figure, it's impossible for the son-of-a-bitch to make a dime on the deal." I've also seen general contractors accept bids at such low prices that they knew a subcontractor would end up in the red or, worse, go broke. There's nothing clever or shrewd about doing business in a way where, going into the deal, you know the other person will get hurt. It's also not in your best interest, because you put yourself at risk that the other party might be forced to cut corners and consequently give you inferior merchandise and poor service. In the case of a subcontractor, in addition to your getting sloppy workmanship, the completion of an entire project could be delayed.

My philosophy is to make deals that are good for both

parties. I want the other guy to walk away from the table saying, "That's the best deal I ever made," and I want to say the same thing. Those *are* the best deals—when both parties think so.

Our franchisees own their own businesses, and like other businesspeople, now and then they may choose to sell their clubs. They do so because they want to retire or venture into another field, they become disinterested, and so on. Our contract with them states that before a sale is made to a third party, it must meet with our approval. One obvious reason is that we don't want to be in business with undesirable and unqualified people. By undesirable, I mean somebody with a shady past, and by unqualified, I mean somebody who lacks the skills to succeed in our business. We're not interested in having a brief affair with the buyer—like a good marriage, we want a long-term relationship. For this reason, we must be very selective about whom a UCC franchise is sold to.

Equally important, if a UCC franchisee's asking price is too high, we won't allow it to be sold to a third party, even though he or she is willing to pay the price. Again, we have to live with the person who buys the franchise, and if that person pays too much for it, he or she might be too indebted right from the start to make a go of the franchise. So we step in to make sure a franchise is sold at a fair price.

## Deliver More than You Promise

I prefer to undersell rather than oversell. From experience, I have learned that underselling always works better. For example, I've made a lot of reservations for car rentals, and with some companies, I've been very pleasantly surprised, while others have disappointed me. With the better automobile agencies, I've been told, "We're sorry, Mr. Gagan, but we have no full-sized cars available, so if you don't object, we can rent you one of our luxury models for the same price." That's a nice surprise.

Then there are those companies that quote low rates via their toll-free reservations numbers, but sock it to you at rental lots. That is *not* a nice surprise. One company added an extra fee for transportation services from the airport to its off-the-beaten-path lots. I was particularly angry when I discovered its full-sized cars were considered intermediate cars by other agencies, its intermediate cars were classified as compacts, and its compacts were subcompacts.

Hotels are also a wonderful source of pleasant and unpleasant surprises. Good hotels give their customers even better accommodations than they anticipated and include free use of a health club, free airport transportation, free in-room movies, and so on. Others charge outrageously high rates for local telephone services, room services, etc. While a company may abuse its customers once, it generally doesn't get a second chance; success rests on referrals and repeat business generated from satisfied customers.

Speaking of pleasant surprises, we have an incentive program for our franchisees in which, depending on sales production, they can receive Cadillacs and Mercedes. In 1989 our franchisees Dan Powell and his brother-in-law, Dave Lappin, qualified for a Cadillac. Dan and Dave are two fine young men in their midtwenties, and they worked hard to earn this car. Scott Powell, who is Dan's older brother, told me how excited they were to have won it, and that they were going with their wives to the local dealer to pick it up.

"Giving one car to two young men isn't such a good idea," I said to Scott. "How are they going to handle sharing a Cadillac?"

"They'll take turns. One guy will use it one month, and one the next," Scott explained.

"That's not good," I said. "You know how much I love these two. Let's call our leasing agent, and we'll give them two identical cars. But we won't tell them. When the two couples go down to pick up the one car, each will get one."

Scott agreed, and, needless to say, Dan and Dave were very pleased to receive two Cadillacs. Everyone likes a nice surprise.

From the outset, I always believed in giving UCC members even more than they bargained for. There was a certain point, for example, when I could have said, "We now have 100 suppliers, and that's certainly enough to satisfy our members." And we could easily have been justified stopping at the point when 200 suppliers were signed up. By making such a decision, we would have cut down on a lot of time, effort, and costs. We were under no obligation to keep adding new suppliers. Instead, however, we continued to expand the number of our manufacturers, and today there are more than 500 suppliers. As long as we're in this business, we will continue to search for ways to offer even more to our members. Someday we'll have 1,000 suppliers, and I can't imagine we'll stop there either.

Another thing: Although we earn no profit when members buy merchandise, we are always encouraging them to use the club. Once we even telephoned several hundred members to find out why they hadn't made a single purchase during the past twelve months.

Our message to these members was: "I'm not pushing you to buy anything. I'm just truly concerned and want you to take advantage of your membership. When you joined, we told you that we cared about you, and we'd do anything we could for you, but you're not coming in. One of two things must have happened. Either we didn't explain the club to you properly and now you don't understand how it works, or perhaps we offended you in some way. Which is it? And what can we do to correct it?"

In the vast majority of cases, people were apologetic and assured us that they had not been offended. Some would say, "You know, I was just talking to my wife about how we need a lawn mower, and I said, 'Doesn't that club we belong to sell lawn mowers? If they do, let's go down and buy one.' We'll probably see you next week."

Although our only motive was to increase customer satisfaction, we took a risk by calling our members. Somebody could have thought, "I suspected UCC was making something when I buy from them, and this confirms it."

During his senior year in college, my son Jamie created a survey for us on his computer. It contained forty-two questions and was sent out to five thousand of our members. We wanted to find out what they were thinking, so the questions ranged from what kind of merchandise we should carry to what their biggest complaints were about UCC. It asked whether they would like us to sell such products as insurance, pharmaceutical goods, and so on. The most common complaint was the length of time they had to wait for the merchandise.

One member wrote in, "I'll tell you what bothers me. I go by your headquarters and see all those fancy foreign cars in your parking lot." Evidently, this man though we must have been making too much money and paying outrageously high salaries to our employees. Now, although UCC makes no money on the sale of merchandise to its members, we do make enough money from the sale of memberships to pay our bills and still show a healthy profit. If we didn't, we wouldn't be in business. I personally wrote back to that man, saying that we operated our business to make a profit, and what's wrong with that? If we didn't make a profit, there would be no UCC.

The survey also provided us with some demographics about our members' income, marital status, and so on. The more we know about them, the better we can serve them.

## Never Compromise a Principle

I'm all for change. In fact, with one exception, everything about a company is subject to change. Corporate names change—IBM was formerly the Computing-Tabulating-Recording Co., Exxon Corp. was the Standard Oil Co., Navistar was International Harvester, and Citicorp was First National City Bank. Locations change—companies move their headquarters from city to city, country to country. Products change—originally Du Pont Co.'s prime business was gunpowder, and Rockwell International Corp., the aerospace company, started out as the maker of parking meters. And, of course, successful corporations "outlive" management, so the management is constantly subject to change.

The single exception that must never be changed is one's principles. To paraphrase Thomas Jefferson, in matters of principle one should stand like a rock; in other matters swim with the current. Another man who thought like Jefferson was Thomas Watson, Jr., the son of the founder of IBM, and a vibrant leader who served as the company's CEO during the 1950s and 1960s, a crucial period for the computer industry. Watson said, "For any organization to survive and achieve success, there must be a sound set of principles on which it bases all its policies and actions. But more important is its faithful adherence to those principles."

The only sacred cow in an organization is its principles. Regardless of its product or size, it must have certain bedrock beliefs that serve as a guiding force to its people and provide strength during times of difficulty. These beliefs must be irrevocable and adhered to throughout the organization.

The principles UCC abides by are: (1) Every individual is treated fairly and respectfully, including customers, employees, and suppliers; (2) We must provide the best possible service; and (3) We must always strive for continuous improvement.

These principles are our strength. Our people understand that this pillar doesn't move. The water might swirl around it, but on matters of principle, the company will not budge. While we work hard at being light on our feet in every other respect, on matters of principle, there is no room for flexibility.

## You Can Never Give Too Much Service

One of IBM's three principles that has dictated the conduct of its employees since 1914 states that they should strive to provide better service than *any* other company in the world. Notice that it doesn't specify that IBM should be the best in its own industry or in its own country!

While obviously there can only be one company that's the best in the world at servicing its customers, UCC also shares this noble ambition. This is a goal that *every* organization should strive to achieve.

In today's competitive society, I don't think a business can survive, let alone succeed, if it is not service-driven. During UCC's early years, the emphasis was initially on the sales effort. We believed that without sales volume there could be no growth, and the company was established on the premise that volume was essential in order to attract major suppliers. It didn't take long before we realized that providing outstanding service must be synonymous with sales effort.

As for every business, our success is dependent upon the goodwill generated through satisfied customers. Referrals only come when members become sincere believers in our concept. To make them believers, we must provide them with so much service they feel guilty when they *don't* refer UCC to their friends. It's not enough to provide thousands of dollars of savings to our members; if they don't get great service, they won't refer people to us. One member once said to me what sums up the sentiment of so many others: "When a close friend of mine told me she and her husband were shopping around for a dining room set retailing at $12,000, I became sick just thinking about them spending their hard-earned money, knowing they would be paying double what it cost at the club. I *had* to get them to join UCC."

While this member stated that his reason for referring a friend to us was based on the good value we offered, I think it was only part of his reason. If we had given him poor service every time he placed an order through us, I'm convinced he never would have recommended us to anyone. In fact, recent studies show that people are willing to pay *more* for good service. Knowing this, it's not enough for us to provide wholesale prices—we must deliver outstanding service too.

As you can see, providing extraordinary service is self-serving, but I have no problem with this motive. Yet there is another reason for doing it. Sales and service must never be separated. Good service is an integral part of the value received from your product. This means it's the right thing to do.

## Leading by Example

Years ago, a young college graduate joined us as a salesperson, later becoming a purchasing agent. One day he came into my office to inform me that upon checking our invoices, he discovered that we were billed for only three sewing machines although we received four. He was quite elated to show me that this bookkeeping error represented a $190 savings to the company. Not wanting to hurt his feelings, I complimented him for his astuteness in picking up such a minute detail. Then I added, "While we can use the money, George, I can't let you do that, because I know how your conscience will bother you. And sleepless nights will be a higher cost to us than the $190 of savings. So I suggest that you call and tell them about the extra unit, and that we'd appreciate having a correct invoice forwarded to us. Besides, we've never been chiselers, and we don't want to start now."

He was not a dishonest person; I think he was just looking for leadership. As I look back, it's probable that he was unconsciously testing me. It's not enough to tell your people to do the right thing. You can only expect them to do it by following your example.

I'm convinced that it's natural for people to want to do the right thing. But they won't when management lets them down. Management can only be effective when it inspires others to exert their best efforts. This is basic stuff. I don't think, however, that people are willing to give their loyalty and devotion to a manager and/or organization that delivers poor value and inferior service to its customers. Imagine what it does to the morale of a worker in an automobile plant who sees shoddy and unsafe cars coming off the line. Or what goes through that worker's mind when his or her friends ridicule the worker for the inferior cars his or her company manufactures. I have to believe it shames the worker and eats away at his or her self-esteem.

In every industry, I'm certain people want to take pride in their work, and they want to be loyal to their employer. But pride and loyalty must never be taken for granted. People aren't automatically proud and loyal simply because they're put on the payroll. A proud and loyal work force must be earned. You earn them on a daily basis by treating employees and customers fairly and respectfully. When you treat others this way, they respond by treating you the same way. This is what good leadership is all about.

# —11—

# YOU WIN WITH PEOPLE

THE PHRASE "people are a company's most valuable asset" has been said so often that the words are trite. Yet, even in today's world of highly advanced technology, the performance of every successful organization *is* a direct result of how effectively its people work together. Study any great corporation, and you'll observe how people—not machinery, real estate, or inventory—are the common denominator that serves as the single determining factor for its success.

In my business, the people who operate each franchise are, indeed, the most significant factor in determining success. In short, each UCC club is only as good as its management. In the beginning, when a franchise failed, blame was placed on everything from the territory to the competition, poor locations to depressed economic conditions. Yet, when a troubled franchise was sold and a new manager took over, its success proved that people, above all else, made the difference. Knowing this, management's number one priority must be the recruiting, training, and development of its people, combined with a never-ending emphasis on maintaining high morale.

In particular, as a service business, UCC is a people business. We have no inventories, nor do we manufacture anything. So if we don't concentrate on our people, there is little else for us to do.

In truth, everything *any* business does depends on human beings. Unlike machines, people have egos and emotional frailties, and, accordingly, they must be treated differently. They require praise and recognition. People also become restless and bored, so they must be given challenges. And they need inspiration. Management must understand these needs, and to do so, it must listen to its people. It must then respond to what it hears. In particular, management must realize that not all people are alike. It is the differences in people that complicate matters.

## Surround Yourself with the Best People

Here, too, what I say is obvious. If people are the most important factor in determining the success of a company, it stands to reason that the best people should be hired. While nobody can argue with this statement, it is easier said than done. First, managers are people, too—and, accordingly, they have their human frailties, one of which is large egos. Most often large egos are a result of low self-esteem and insecurity. As a consequence, a manager often feels threatened having somebody on the payroll who might outperform and outshine him or her.

Second, during its infancy a business often can't afford to hire the best people. If it were not for these two factors, I believe the competition to attract the best people would be incredibly fierce. So let us be thankful that there are managers who do have big egos, because, as a result, those companies that can well afford to hire top people generally do not. Consequently, there is no need to worry about the billion-dollar corporations monopolizing the best-people market.

With limited funds, I was unable to hire expensive people, so initially I had to settle for some less-than-adequate help. It was only through a stroke of sheer luck that Fred Wittlinger and Jack Allen came aboard. These two men defy the saying "Eagles don't flock, you have to find them one at a time." I also could never have hired either of them on a straight salary. The attraction to them was the opportunity to own their own business.

It was about a year after they acquired a franchise in Valparaiso that Fred joined me on a full-time basis in the capacity of vice president. Prior to that, he and Jack had been working their franchise in the evenings. Fred was still an IBM rep, and Jack was an attorney. To persuade Fred to join me as a salaried employee, I added $1,000 to the top earnings he received from IBM. "It took you eight years to make this salary with them, and I'm starting you off at more in your first year with UCC." Considering that I drew out $4,000 in salary during *my* first year, Fred was very well paid. Today, he's the chairman of the board, and Jack is president, and their salaries are comparable to those earned by the heads of Fortune 500 companies. Neither one has ever asked me for a raise.

It's a serious mistake for a business owner to begrudge paying people well—in particular, commissioned salespeople. During the early years, I had franchisees with earnings that surpassed mine—and I was delighted. The more they made, the better it was for the company. Yet I've witnessed many sales managers, vice presidents, and even CEOs who became enraged when a commissioned sales rep made more money than they. What happens is that the managers' egos got in their way; they couldn't cope with having somebody in a subordinate position outearn them. So what did they do? They cut commission schedules, reduced the size of the rep's territory, and, in the process, they ruined the morale of their entire sales organization. I could never understand their motive. After all, they signed an agreement with the rep to pay *x* amount of commissions, which was built into their costs of doing business. As I said, the more the rep makes, the more it benefits the company. If anything, managers should reward their top salesperson for doing such outstanding work, not penalize him or her.

If necessary, a small-business owner must be prepared to make short-term sacrifices by reducing his or her salary in order to pay more to attract key people. Believe me, in the long run, it's a wise investment. I realize that most small-business people operate on a shoestring, so it's a difficult decision to hire expensive people. But hire them you must—and the same applies to hiring top professional services of attorneys, accountants, and so on. I believe in bringing in the best professional talent; this is no place for a businessperson to skimp.

Over the years, I have discovered that there are vast differences between run-of-the-mill and top professionals. Contrary to what many people believe, there is an enormous variance in their skills. It's ridiculous to think all professional people have similar ability. Yet I've seen patients randomly select a surgeon to perform surgery where the outcome can be life or death. "What's the difference?" they say. "A doctor is a doctor. They all go to medical school and study the same books." Perhaps, but 50 percent of them graduated in the bottom half of their class. If an intelligent approach isn't taken in the selection of a surgeon, imagine how these same people choose an accountant or attorney.

Over the years, I have observed that the skills of CPAs and attorneys are not all alike. To think that they are is like thinking all tennis players, golfers, and basketball players, professionals and amateurs alike, perform at about the same level in their respective sports. As an example of how the talent of accountants may vary, note that in a 1990 survey conducted by *Money* magazine, fifty tax preparers were asked to do a sample tax return for a hypothetical family of four. Only two of the fifty received a perfect score. The rest had different answers for the tax liability. Their answers ranged from $9,806 to $21,216, while the correct amount was $12,038. Their fees ranged from $271 to $4,000. As you can see, the level of performance is not identical with all professional people in any field.

## How to Recruit Good People

The companies that do the best job of recruiting good people are the ones that give recruitment a high priority. Unlike those organizations that leave the hiring to lower-echelon managers, they get their top managers involved. These executives believe that the selection of people is simply too important to be delegated. After all, if a company starts out with an inferior work force, two strikes are automatically against it. There's a lot of wisdom in the words "No matter how much training you give an ol' gray mare, it ain't ever going to win the Kentucky Derby."

A lesson that American corporations can learn from the Japanese is the thoroughness and extensive effort with which they recruit people. In mid-1978, when Honda, the first of the Japanese "transplants," began building its automobile plant in the United States, the company was determined to select the "right" associates. More than three thousand applications poured into its Marysville, Ohio, plant. One hundred workers were hired. The three key recruiters were Honda's top three plant executives. Their recruiting chores were tedious and time-consuming, but Honda well understood that these first hundred hand-picked individuals would serve as the nucleus that later would expand into a large work force. So they didn't take shortcuts. Unlike the typical brief interviews conducted by domestic automakers hiring production workers, the Honda interview lasted for approximately one hour. Those candidates asked back were subjected to more interviews, often meeting with two or three top managers. Because some of the applicants had daytime jobs, the Honda recruiting team conducted interviews during the evenings and on Saturdays. With an effort like this, it is no wonder that the Marysville Honda plant, with a work force in excess of 10,000 today, is considered one of the most productive automobile manufacturing facilities in the world. Incidentally, when Nissan, Toyota, and Mazda came to America to assemble cars, similar efforts were exhibited in their hiring programs.

When people are randomly hired without selectivity, a

company pays a heavy toll. This is applicable to manufacturing, sales, servicing—all fields. If people are a company's most valuable asset, management must pay the price up front by investing its time and money in its hiring efforts. If not, the price inevitably will be higher down the road.

The majority of our people were referrals or people we knew beforehand, not recruited from newspaper ads or employment agencies. Home office employees have referred their friends and relatives to us. And some excellent employees started out in our summer internship program. One of our best sources of franchisees is members. About two-thirds of our franchise owners began their relationship with UCC as members of a club. They became so enthusiastic about our concept that they inquired about a franchise. As a result, we now actively mail literature to our club members, inviting them to inquire about owning a franchise.

For example, June and Larry Grossman joined our Fairfield, New Jersey, club in November 1987. From the beginning, June thought UCC was the greatest concept since sliced bread. At first, Larry, a successful Wall Street stockbroker in his midthirties, was skeptical. If it hadn't been for his wife's insistence, they would never have become members. June's enthusiasm, however, slowly won him over. In January 1988, she convinced Larry that they should visit our home office to meet with Scott Powell, our franchise coordinator. Larry liked what he saw, and in February, June became a director in our Fairfield club. That May, when they attended our conference in Chicago, Larry made the decision that he would leave Wall Street and the two of them would acquire a franchise. The Grossmans operate a very successful franchise today in Westchester County, New York, and they love their new careers. As Larry says, "I'm not under the stress I endured in the securities field. The ups and downs in the market had far too many uncertainties."

When it comes to hiring people you don't know well, I strongly advise you to thoroughly investigate them. Good people aren't afraid to have you check references; in fact, they welcome it. So take the time to contact former employees, schools and colleges, and even neighbors and other acquaintances. Don't be shy about asking an interviewee who claims he had $x$ amount of earnings for the past two years to furnish you with copies of his income tax returns. I can't tell you how many horror stories I've heard over the years about people who made wonderful impressions during an interview but turned out to have a record as long as your arm. It's serious business to hire the right people, so make the effort to check them out.

## If It's Not Good for Your People, It's Not Good for You

I have a very simple rule. I think in terms of what's in the best interests of my people, and I act accordingly. This doesn't mean that I do what's right for them to my detriment. Instead, I find some common ground that permits me to do what's beneficial for both of us. And if it's something that's really exceptional for an employee, even though I don't benefit, I'll do it anyhow.

Admittedly, it's sometimes hard to make such a decision. For example, in April 1976, I was faced with a tough one. At the time, Fred and Jack were vice presidents and my two top executives. As I mentioned earlier, Jack was practicing law when he joined UCC. In his earlier days, he served as a city court judge in Valparaiso and, at the time, was the youngest in the city's history. In 1976, Jack was asked to accept an appointment by the governor and serve as a superior court judge. It was something he had wanted to do all of his life, so he came to discuss the offer with me. My first reaction was, "Do you realize how much I have invested in you? We've built a good business, and if you leave, how can I replace you?"

Jack responded by telling me that he would acquiesce to my wishes. I told him I'd sleep on it and get back to him by the end of the week. At first, I could only think about how losing him would be an insurmountable setback to the company. The more I thought about it, however, the more I realized there was a shortage of truly competent judges and how exceptional Jack would be. I contemplated having him leave UCC, and I recalled the times when I had said that, unlike England, the United States political system does not attract our best statesmen. The same applies to our bench. Then it dawned on me that I had an opportunity to contribute something to our society—*Jack*. I knew he was an extremely honorable person, and I was certain he'd be a fine judge. I also knew how this judgeship would be the fulfillment of his lifetime dream.

When we met again, I said, "Jack, do it, and you have my blessing. I also want you to understand that you are not leaving anything behind that you can't pick up. There is an open door for you at UCC as long as we are here. I'm proud of you, and I know you'll be a wonderful judge."

Jack took the appointment and did an outstanding job for more than five years. In 1981, he rejoined us. Seven years later, I named him president of UCC, and Fred became our chairman of the board.

Somehow, when you make your people your number one priority, it all comes back to you. I suppose it's human nature for people to respond in kind when they're treated with respect. I'm sure it's because they are appreciative, and one thing is certain: they'll be more loyal to a manager who's decent and fair with them than to one who's always looking for ways to exploit them. When you care for them, they'll reciprocate.

## Your People Deserve First-Class Treatment

It was at the May 1988 UCC conference when Jack and Fred officially received their promotions. Instead of simply shuffling some papers and giving them new titles, I wanted to make it a special event. After all, they were so deserving, and on their leadership rested the future of the organization. So, on the Saturday night of a three-day conference in Chicago, we had a black-tie affair in the Hyatt's main ballroom. A professional party organizer decorated the room in a magnificent black-and-white art deco motif, and the Tommy Dorsey band was hired for the evening. The invitation was delivered in an elaborate package that contained a silver platter. Each club had to meet certain quotas in order to qualify its employees and their spouses, and only the top achievers could attend. All expenses at the convention would be paid by the company.

Almost one thousand people attended what we billed as the Inauguration Ball. I announced to the organization that I had never attended high school, and consequently I missed out on my prom. This ball would be *my prom night*. I had the pleasure of introducing our two guests of honor, and I formally congratulated Fred and Jack on their promotions to their new positions. It was an evening filled with deep emotion—and a night all who attended are unlikely to forget. The big band music from the 1940s and 1950s had the whole room swaying, and although the band was scheduled to leave at twelve-thirty, I had them stay an extra hour because the crowd was having such a good time.

It was an expensive party and worth every penny. There's no place I'd rather spend my money than on my people. And when I do, I believe in treating them to the best. At past conventions, we've had such entertainers as the Beach Boys, Kool and the Gang, the Fifth Dimension, the Commodores, and the Gatlin Brothers. Our guest speakers have included Earl Nightingale, Zig Ziglar, Paul Harvey, Bobby Knight, Mike Ditka, and Vice President Dan Quayle.

When it comes to entertaining my employees, I'd rather go first class with them or not at all. When I take them to dinner, it's always to one of the best restaurants in town, and whether I give them tickets to the theater or a ball game, it's always a front-row seat. This doesn't mean I don't keep an eye on expenses. I do, just as I'm sure every effective CEO does. However, there are certain areas where being frugal is destructive to morale, and that's where I draw the line.

It appalls me when I see companies cut corners and treat their people like second-class citizens. Not long ago a young executive for a medium-sized patio furniture manufacturer flew in from Los Angeles to visit our Merrillville headquarters. She met with me at nine-thirty in the morning, and during the course of the conversation, I asked her if she had been able to find a decent restaurant in the area for her supper the night before.

"I ate in LA," she said. "I took the red-eye flight."

"You must be exhausted."

"Yeah, but it comes with the territory," she said. "Our company is on a tight austerity program, and only our top management flies East the day before. By coming on the red-eye, I saved the company $200 on my tickets, plus another $150 for dinner and lodging."

I started to calculate what time she had left the night before. She must have left at two o'clock in the morning Central Standard Time and arrived at O'Hare around 6:00 A.M. It would have taken her another two hours to grab breakfast, rent a car, and drive to our offices. That meant she had an hour and a half to kill, probably sleeping in her car or reading the newspaper. The poor woman was so washed out she was having difficulty conversing with me. While the company saved some money, it did so at her expense. As a consequence, she was unable to function effectively during our meeting, and the wear and tear on her also had a price tag. In my opinion, it was the wrong place to reduce expenses, and it had to have a devastating effect on her morale. I was especially sickened to be told that the top management always traveled first class.

I've seen other companies cut corners by sticking their middle managers in cubbyholes while top managers have large, lavishly decorated offices. While I have no objection to elaborate executive offices, I don't think it's wise for there to be such disparity. For the same reason, I don't like fancy executive dining rooms unless there is adequate eating space for company rank-and-file employees. For the record, I have nothing against perks provided to those who have worked their way up the corporate ladder. I think there is a place for this sort of recognition. But I do object to flaunting it to such a degree that it causes dissension between the haves and the have-nots within the organization.

## Getting People Involved

The terms *employee involvement* and *workers' involvement* are buzzwords in management circles today. And while volumes of articles and books have been written about the subject, it all boils down to communicating with your people. But remember, communication is a two-way street. You must inform them about what's going on, *and* you must listen to what they have to tell you. Then, by listening carefully and finding out what they think is wrong or right, you must respond by implementing changes. Otherwise you are just engaging in rhetoric.

People need to feel needed. They want to feel that they are making a contribution. This is true from the executive suite to the mail room. I don't think anyone, if given a choice, wants to walk through life without leaving some sort of a footprint. Even the guy in the shipping department wants to take pride in his work for having the best shipping department. It's up to management to recognize this basic need of people, and when they deserve it, you must praise them for their good work. When you do, they will respond by doing an even better job. People want to take pride in their work, but you must let them.

One effective way to motivate people is to get them involved. There's an old saying, "People will support that which they help to create." This makes a lot of sense to me. If you communicate to them what you plan to achieve in the beginning stages of a project, ask them for their ideas, and then listen to their feedback, they are more likely to be supportive, because they have participated in the decision-making process. Not only have you boosted their morale, they'll supply you with some valuable information that could contribute to the achievement of your objective.

I also believe in communicating the bad news as well as the

good news. While an announcement that your company suffered record losses the previous year isn't reason for celebra-
tion, not having anything to say about it is bound to cause
some anxiety among the troops. I believe in facing a problem
squarely in the eye, so in 1977 when we had our worst year
ever, I made no attempt to keep it a secret. If I had, it would
have had a devastating effect on morale, because I'm sure
everybody in administration was aware that the company was
doing poorly. So, at a January meeting attended by our home
office people, my message was, "We lost a lot of money last
year, and thankfully we learned a lot in the process. So let's
bury our mistakes and do what we must to turn this thing
around." Because I leveled with them, even that negative news
had a positive effect on everyone's morale.

It's a serious mistake for management to keep its work
force in the dark when things are going badly. It is particularly foolish in the case of a publicly owned corporation,
because, in only a matter of time, annual statements are
released to the general public. What's most damaging to
morale is when management fails to tell employees, who later
hear the bad news from an outsider or read about it in the
newspapers. When this happens, employees are embarrassed
and hurt; they're hurt because their company didn't think
they were important enough to know before the general
public.

## A Fish-or-Cut-Bait Philosophy

One word I'd like to eliminate from every UCC manager's
vocabulary when describing people is *potential*. I am well
aware that the training of new young employees makes them
more effective. I understand that people can improve at their
work. What exasperates me, however, is when an individual is
given every opportunity to succeed, but he or she makes few
or no contributions whatsoever. There comes a time when an
employee who's not carrying his or her weight must be let go.
But often, rather than facing up to it, a manager pleads, "But
he has potential." In truth, the manager probably knows the

employee has failed to perform, but he or she wants to avoid the painful admission that the wrong person was hired. Or the manager might, in fact, like the employee and not want to hurt him or her. In business, however, there's an obligation to do what's right for the entire organization, and painful decisions are often essential. In the long run, a person who doesn't fit in your company will be better off somewhere else.

All too often I hear excuses that "so-and-so has gotten off to a slow start, but give him some more time and he'll turn the corner." Of course it depends on how much time is involved, but after a while, if somebody hasn't succeeded, the chances are that person is never going to make the grade. The more time that transpires waiting to see if the employee is going to make it, the more it costs the organization. That's why I say it's vital to know when to fish and when to cut bait.

## No Crown Princes

My son Jack is our vice president of merchandising. He does an excellent job, and I'm very proud of him. Jack started in the business working on the loading dock while he was in high school. Needless to say, he's come a long way during the past nineteen years.

Since I own one hundred percent of the company, some people might suspect Jack is a sure thing to someday be CEO. If he's the best person for the job at the time, he will be. But there are no crown princes at UCC. I've witnessed many unqualified sons and daughters get promoted over qualified people, and I think it's a gross injustice. First, it can be a costly blunder that can wreck a business. There's no end to the damage the wrong person can do.

Second, it wrecks the morale of the entire organization. It sends a message to all employees that no matter how well anyone performs, he or she can advance only so far in the organization. This is particularly true in a family business with many relatives on the payroll. When promotions are given to incapable family members, those who are capable are the first to abandon ship. As a result, the company loses its best people. This compounds the problem, because when a company is drained of its top managers, even an effective CEO is severely handicapped.

Third, when a company owner taps unqualified offspring for a top spot, it places tremendous pressure on the young person to perform—and that's not fair. Not only is this person frustrated by his or her inadequacies, when he or she does fail, the young person feels guilty about letting down employees and the family as well. If a parent truly loves his or her offspring, the parent wouldn't promote the child to a position in which he or she is destined to fail.

## A Few Words About Nepotism

Many leading companies have nepotism policies that forbid the employment of relatives. These companies are concerned that people who are not qualified will be put on the payroll. Or perhaps management wants to avoid a situation where one employee's relative is accepted for employment while another's is not. Hence, a good way to elude some nasty politicking is to never hire a relative of any employee, even family members of the owner! If so, this eliminates the need to worry about a would-be crown prince.

While these are the typical reasons for having a nepotism policy, I'm opposed to one. My reason is that I oppose any form of discrimination. In this case, it's a policy that penalizes anyone who happens to be a relative of an owner or employee. In some instances, a large company may be the biggest employer in the community. Such an example is the Honda Motor Company's plant in Marysville, Ohio, a town with a population of 8,400, less than the number of employees who work at the plant. Honda does not permit members of the same family to work at the plant. Its reason is an unusual one: by eliminating the employment of spouses and children of the same household, the company enables more families to be involved with the company. This is in line with Honda's commitment to serve the entire community.

Although one can make a good case for a nepotism policy,

I still think the cons outweigh the pros. Over the years, some of our best people have been related to UCC employees, so I'd hate to think that as a result of an existing company policy, we would have had to pass on these people. There's also a valid explanation why family members are likely to become a company's star performers. These people grow up in an atmosphere where they're exposed to a parent's, uncle's, sibling's, or other relative's enthusiasm for his or her employer, and they receive a good education about the company and its industry. As a result, a son, for example, chooses to follow in his father's footsteps. I think that's terrific, and such a person is an excellent candidate to hire. It's a shame to automatically reject him because he was born to the "wrong" parent.

## Promotions from Within

It's a sign of weakness when a company fails to promote people from within and must constantly go outside to hire its management. It demonstrates that the company lacks the capacity to develop its own people for advancement. Perhaps as devastating as the crown prince syndrome, bringing in an outsider wrecks morale. People think, "It doesn't matter how hard I work for the promotion, the company will bring in somebody from the outside anyway."

For this reason, an organization must have a system in which it can provide advancement for those who perform. If it doesn't, it's a sure bet that its best people are going to seek employment elsewhere. A drain of this nature will stifle a company's growth. An exodus of enough good people can even cause a company's demise.

At UCC, our salespeople are offered a carrot that provides them with several opportunities to move into management. And, of course, the carrot that most motivates our star performers is the attainment of their own franchise. Our franchisees who build successful clubs may then want bigger challenges. So they can expand their horizons by opening additional clubs.

Lynn Lutz is one of our success stories. Lynn was only

twenty-one years old in 1974 when she became a merchandise center representative at our South Bend club. (The position of merchandise center representative is of no small import in our business. These people are the ones responsible for keeping all the promises our sales reps make.) Her weekly salary was $120. Within a couple of months, Lynn was asked if she'd like to make some extra money by selling memberships. She accepted and began making calls to prospects at their homes on weekends. Before long her commissions were averaging around $500 a week in addition to her $120 salary. Eventually, she became a full-time salesperson and did a super job. In 1979 her boyfriend and now husband, David Lutz, had been working as an assistant foreman in a factory in Elkhart, and it didn't take long before he wanted a job with UCC, too. At first, Lynn rejected the idea because she feared that if he didn't succeed, it might jeopardize their relationship. David persisted, however ("I was impressed that she owned her own home and a Cadillac," he recalls), joined the South Bend sales force, and, like Lynn, also did well. Lynn and David were married in 1980, and after having worked as senior directors, they became franchisees in Columbus, Ohio. Today they enjoy six-figure incomes.

## Letting Go of the Reins

"The secret of my success is that I surround myself with people who are smarter than I" has been said by many great business leaders. But there's little use in having bright employees unless you are willing to let them participate in the decision-making process. You won't hold on to them—no matter how much they're paid—if they're not allowed to think. Only a fool hires top-quality people yet fails to give them the room they need to take charge. I derive great delight in having a management team that I know can run my business in my absence. As a consequence, I spend the winter months in Palm Desert, California, confident that UCC is in good hands.

When top people are hired, it's essential to have faith in

their skills, especially in those areas in which you have no expertise. For example, prior to joining UCC in 1982, our vice president of finance, Jim Gillies, was a CPA with a large Canadian conglomerate. I brought him aboard because, back then, while our financial condition was stable, our accounting department was quite primitive, and our computer systems were not integrated. Well, he turned things around, and we now have a smooth operation.

I had to trust his judgment, or he couldn't have created our present systems. When he presented a program to me that would fix things, I didn't understand the details, but I was willing to OK the large sum of money required to implement it. As a result, our accounting department runs like clockwork today. Jim even set up an internal audit department that audits every UCC club at least once every eighteen months. We have a traveling audit staff of three people who are all business school graduates, and they spend a majority of their time on the road visiting our franchises. The franchisees are very supportive of these activities because, as salespeople, their strong suit is definitely not administrative work. Jim has since established a standard accounting manual, which enables franchisees to furnish us quarterly financial reports. In a million years, I couldn't have straightened out our accounting problems as Jim did. And fortunately, I didn't have to, because I was able to let go of the accounting reins and have Jim take them over.

## The Magic of a Proprietary Interest

I've heard a lot of sales managers deliver pep talks telling their reps, "The company needs your sales production. We're counting on you to go out there and generate more business." While get-one-for-the-Gipper pep talks have some merit, what I think is really important to understand is that a salesperson is motivated to sell for one person: him- or herself. When a salesperson goes home after a long, hard day's work in the field, the one important thought racing through his or her mind is, "I got mine today!" The salesperson didn't do it for the company, the sales manager, or anyone else, and anybody who thinks differently doesn't understand what drives people to succeed. This doesn't mean a person doesn't care about his or her employer—it's a matter of priorities. And in this area, each of us looks out for number one.

It's easy to relate this to a commissioned salesperson. After all, this person's paycheck is dependent upon how well he or she performs. Every salesperson has a proprietary interest in his or her work. But how does a company motivate its hourly and salaried people? There are ways. One is by paying people piecemeal; another is via a profit-sharing plan that rewards them for their performance. If the company does well and generates good earnings, employees participate in those profits. And, of course, the payment of bonuses is still another effective tool to reward employees for their individual efforts. In each case, the individual has an incentive to excel because he or she is rewarded by the success of the company.

I don't think there's anything that motivates a person more than giving him or her a piece of the action. A person who has a stake in ownership is going to have a better attitude than the one who works for somebody else. In addition to the pride that comes with ownership, there's the risk factor. When someone's own money is on the line, it's bound to make that person care more about the bottom line—especially when his or her own effort will determine whether its color is black or red.

There was a period when UCC had a rather high turnover of franchise managers, which, in part, was caused by a lack of proprietary interest on the part of the managers. This happened in the mid-1970s, when we stopped selling franchises and instead opened company-owned clubs that were operated by managers. There were also incidents in which some franchises were run by absentee management because franchisees had either opened another club or simply become complacent. Although the hired managers were well trained and experienced as top sales producers, our turnover of these people was remarkably high.

In early 1983, I was having lunch with Scott Powell, a

young man whom I met when he caddied for me at our country club. We recalled how we first met and that later he had gone away to college and worked as a salesperson in our Terre Haute club. Scott made so much money in the summer that he wanted to quit college and work for us full-time, but I insisted that his education come first and assured him that there would be plenty of time afterward to join the company. However, by the time Scott graduated, he had other ambitions. His mind was set on working for a Fortune 500 company, and, sure enough, he landed a sales job with Owens-Corning Fiberglass. Scott had been employed by Owens for two years.

We reminisced before ordering lunch, and I asked him, "Are you happy with your work?"

Scott expressed that his real desire was to own his own business, and if he had the money, he would.

"How much money do you have to invest in a business?"

"Five thousand dollars," he replied.

Once again, it was a napkin on which I began writing down numbers showing how he could become a UCC franchise owner, and I'd be his partner. I made him a deal he couldn't refuse. Unlike other franchisees, he wouldn't have to invest any money. Instead, I would put up everything—the franchise fees, the start-up costs, the capitalization of a newly formed corporation, etc. In turn, Scott would learn our business by enrolling in our management training school, which every new franchisee attends. Afterward, we'd find a location, and he'd receive commissions based on the club's sales volume. It was agreed that the initial profit of the club would go to me to pay back my investment, and after that, we'd share the profits on a fifty-fifty basis. Then we set up a formula whereby if Scott's club averaged fifty memberships a month, or 1,800 in three years, he'd receive 50 percent of the stock in that franchise. This entire transaction took less than five minutes, and we shook hands on it.

That March, Scott and I opened a club in Lombard, a suburb west of Chicago. He had just turned twenty-four. In April, the club's twenty-fifth month, the 1,800th member was enrolled, and Scott received his half ownership in the franchise. That same month, Scott started a second club in Libertyville, Illinois, with a new partner, his older brother, Jack.

In retrospect, my lunch with Scott was an important UCC milestone. It was the beginning of our most innovative tool for future growth: our Management Equity Program (MEP). Basically, this program was developed to enable franchisees to promote people within their organization, with no resources to invest in a franchise, to buy into one. The franchisee who invests the initial sums required to get the new franchise running gets 50 percent of the stock in the new franchise. This program has since been expanded, and now our home office people can also have a proprietary interest in a franchise. Not only does this give them an incentive to recruit top people for a franchise, it provides them with a piece of indirect ownership in UCC. Because the business is privately owned, and until we do go public, this is my way for my management team to accumulate some equity. At the time of this writing, there are fifteen MEP franchises, and more are opening every year. Several of our home office people have interests in an MEP franchise, including Fred Wittlinger, Jack Allen, Rod Troutman, and as I previously mentioned, Scott Powell. In addition to his older brother Jack, coming into the business via an MEP-sponsored franchise with Scott, so have his younger brother, Dan, and his brother-in-law, David Lappin.

The Management Equity Program reduces our turnover because top salespeople with ambition for bigger and better things can obtain ownership in a franchise. Without this carrot, we'd eventually lose them, because they'd seek opportunities elsewhere. I love to challenge our sales force at conferences: "Why are you sitting there telling me how good you are? You boast how many sales you've made, and still you don't have your own club? Look at our people who have their own clubs. A lot of them were never as good as you when they were in the field. What are you waiting for? Come and talk to me about it. If you want to own a club, I will put my money where my mouth is. I'll finance your new club. If you're as good as you think you are, and you *really* believe you are, I'll believe it, too."

Undoubtedly, a big drawing card for a UCC career is the opportunity to obtain a franchise and own a business. This attraction enables us to compete favorably with Fortune 500 companies for the top people. Two such people are May Ling Lai and her husband, Bruce Cerrito. In her late twenties, May had a promising career with Drexel Burnham Lambert, and Bruce was a successful broker with Prudential-Bache. Both worked in the Manhattan area. Bruce and Larry Grossman had worked together on Wall Street, and the two couples were close friends. The Grossman's franchise was doing so well in Westchester that their enthusiasm was contagious. It spread to May and Bruce, who decided to investigate for themselves to "find out if UCC was for real." They conducted extensive research on our company and, consequently, while in Chicago at a wedding, drove to Merrillville to check us out. They liked what they saw.

UCC liked what we saw, too, so we conducted our own investigation of them, and when May and Bruce agreed to purchase a UCC franchise, we invited them to attend our Management Training School, an extensive four-week crash course to prepare new franchisees to operate a club. In January 1989, they enrolled in MTS. Their game plan was for Bruce to attend for only a week, while May would stay for the entire session. Later, he would keep his job on Wall Street while she ran the franchise, although he would work with her in the evenings and on weekends. Finally, once the new club was on its feet, he would join her on a full-time basis. Unfortunately, May became ill, and although she completed her MTS training, she missed a significant number of classes. As a consequence, we didn't feel they were ready for a franchise and encouraged them to delay their decision to purchase one.

May was heartbroken, but she realized that we were looking out for their best interests. A very determined woman, she worked as a director for the Grossmans' Westchester franchise for ten months and did an outstanding job. In January 1990,

May and Bruce opened their own franchise in Nassau County on Long Island, New York. He has since come aboard on a full-time basis, and I am happy to report they are prospering.

Much of our success has resulted from giving people an ownership position—it's a powerful incentive that inspires them to think and work at a much higher level. Every innovative businessperson can do what I've done to give and consequently get the most from his or her people.

# —12—
# Twenty-Four
# Additional Secrets
# to Success

Somewhere deeply ingrained in the back of my brain, something drives me to always deliver more for the money. Herein lies my inspiration for including this final chapter. Here are twenty-four secrets to success. Each by itself is worth many times more than the price of a good book, including this one.

## —NUMBER 1—
### Your First Loss Is Your Best Loss

There's an old expression that you should never throw good money after bad money. I concur. When a venture begins to lose money, a businessperson is wise to cut his or her losses by aborting the enterprise, rather than to invest more money in what is a losing cause. As an investor in the stock market, I might buy a stock at $30 a share, for example, and when its price drops to $28, I'll sell at a $2 loss rather than risk more loss. My decision is based on thinking there is a reason why the price of the stock went down, and unless I know about some positive news on why the price should advance, I'd rather bite the bullet with a known loss than risk a potentially greater loss.

I apply this rule to people, too. If a new employee who looked good when hired turns out to have some serious flaws after a reasonable length of time, I prefer to admit we have erred and discharge the employee while it's still early in the game. I object to procrastinating the unpleasantness of firing somebody once it becomes apparent it must be done. Prolonging the agony only makes matters worse.

## —NUMBER 2—
### Quality Doesn't Cost More, It Saves More

The Japanese industry knows it—but why is American industry taking so long to realize it? *Quality pays.* While in the short run it may cost more money to build quality into your product, in the long run, even more money is saved. A manufacturer's assembly line, for instance, might necessitate an investment in equipment and training, but eventually the savings in terms of eliminating future service calls for repairs, paying off warranties, and settling liability claims may far exceed the costs of a quality program.

Likewise, when you buy any product—whether it's an automobile, a computer, or a dishwashing machine—in determining the best value, you should consider which will be most durable and require the fewest repairs. Then, too, there's a cost you must put on down time. When a computer system breaks down and employees can't function properly, it's costing the company a lot of money. There's also the cost involved that results from lost customers.

## —NUMBER 3—
### There Are Few Victims Who Fail—
### but Many Volunteers

When a business venture fails, it is rare when somebody does not cry how he or she was a victim of uncontrollable events.

Excuses are expressed, such as, "I had a bad location," "I was undercapitalized," "The competition was underselling me," "The economy went sour," "My employees were stealing from me," and, "The business demanded more time than I was willing to give it."

I've seen so many businesses go belly-up whose demise was so predictable. The owner failed because he or she wasn't willing to pay the price that success demands. The owner didn't make a firm commitment to his or her business.

Businesses don't fail. People fail. Some are not willing to make the sacrifice required to succeed. They aren't victims— *they volunteered to fail.*

## —NUMBER 4—
### Being Perfect Will Slow You Down

I am in favor of exerting a best effort. However, sometimes people strive for perfection to a fault. In business, there is often a point when additional spending is not cost-effective because the additional rewards don't warrant it. Simply illustrated, the publishing of an annual report might cost $x$ amount of dollars, and the additional benefit derived from spending an extra 40 percent to include such features as full color and a superior grade of paper does not justify the added expense.

On a national scale, the government might pass legislation requiring the automobile industry to improve fuel efficiency and produce engines that are free of air pollutants. The cost of the technology to accomplish this worthy goal, however, might be so enormous that the expense passed on to the consumer becomes prohibitive. As a consequence, many Americans may no longer be able to afford a new-car purchase. Similarly, the military might overspend for an improved weapon that has the capacity to destroy the enemy several times more than an existing weapon. While the proposed weapon is superior, its increased capacity does nothing to improve the nation's security.

As you can see, although it is noble to strive for perfection, its implementation does not necessarily serve the best interests of a company, the consumer, or society. Still, there are other situations in which if you don't invest money to seek improvement, you'll lose valuable ground with the competition. Since there is only so much money a business can justifiably spend, what is enough and what is too much are difficult decisions.

## —NUMBER 5—
### Good Leaders Are So Scarce, I'm Following Myself

Early in my career, I observed that the vast majority of people don't want to lead—they want somebody they can follow. I think people choose to follow because they think less risk is involved. The leader must be a decision maker, which, in turn, requires risk taking. People prefer to avoid decision making because, as I explained earlier, it puts them in a position where they must risk making a *bad* decision.

If given a choice, however, I prefer to lead. Why? For starters, leaders get paid better than followers. Second, I have always wanted to make a difference. For a leader, both ambitions are attainable.

## —NUMBER 6—
### One Sure Way to Determine the
### Well-Being of a Company

There's a whole slew of ways to analyze a company. But one quick and sure way to make a determination of its well-being is by taking a good look at the turnover of its people. If an organization can't hold on to its people, something's wrong. Either it's not treating them properly, or it doesn't offer them opportunity—so they leave.

Observing the turnover of personnel serves as an excellent barometer, whether you're seeking a new career, looking for a good investment, or wanting to acquire a company. When good people are leaving, something is seriously wrong. And as they say, "A company is only as good as the people it keeps."

## —NUMBER 7—
## Democracy Works Best in Government
## but Poorly in Business

Democracy is the best form of government in the world. Just how superior it is to its antagonist, communism, has been well documented with the turn of events in the Soviet Union, China, and Eastern Europe in 1989–1990. Yet, however noble are the principles of democracy in government, they are not applicable in business. The majority of employees don't vote at the end of the year to determine the pay scales of management and the work force. Nor do the workers of a company collectively decide who shall be the company's officers for the following year. Our free-enterprise system provides the right and opportunity for everybody to have ownership. But those having the most ownership have the right to govern what they own.

It should be noted that a CEO may make a decision that is not shared by the majority of employees, yet that decision may still be the best for the company. A good manager is not required to make popular decisions, but he or she must be decisive.

## —NUMBER 8—
## When You're Wrong, You're Wrong

Nobody is perfect, and everyone makes mistakes. Those who don't make mistakes never take risks, and it is the risk takers in an organization who are its most valuable contributors. What I have just espoused is old hat in management circles. For years, it has been documented that *good managers do make mistakes.* Even so, too many of them have difficulty admitting when they make mistakes. For the most part, it's because they let their pride get in their way.

False pride is a dangerous thing. Rather than trying to bury a mistake, it is far better to say, "I was wrong," and explain what went haywire. Some people think that had Richard Nixon made such a confession during the early stages of Watergate, the public would have reacted differently and he would have finished out his second term as President. He elected, however, to deny any wrongdoing, and this, I believe, eventually led to his resignation.

When you are wrong, the longer you wait to admit it, the more damage is done. And it is far better for a person to be the one to make public his or her own mistake than to have it revealed by somebody else. When it is inevitable that a faux pas will be exposed, it is foolish for the faulty party to attempt to cover it up. Interestingly, when you beat the other person to the punch by confessing your error, it's likely that he or she will accept it in good spirits. A salesperson, for example, might inform a customer that he incorrectly quoted a delivery date. The customer understands and forgives the mistake; however, had the salesperson not called, the buyer might have become irate when the merchandise failed to be delivered on time.

During our four-week crash course at our Management Training School, we discuss many of the things we previously did that failed. "Mistakes are good ideas that didn't work," future franchisees are told. "We want you to know some of the ones we had that looked good but weren't." Illustrating things that went wrong is a good way to teach, so we tell them about how we once tried to give complimentary memberships to VIPs in the community. "Our thinking was based on how a town mayor, for example, who received a free membership would talk us up at dinner parties and banquets. However, we discovered that when a membership is given away for free, and the recipient never hears our sales presentation, he doesn't understand how the club really works. Consequently, he doesn't use it, so when he is asked about UCC, he says, 'It wasn't anything I would ever pay for.' For this reason, we oppose comps—it was a good idea, but it doesn't work."

## —NUMBER 9—
### Use the Right Quote at the Right Time

I remember sitting in on a board meeting where fourteen

people were trying to make a decision. A particular issue was being hotly debated, and finally somebody spoke out: "I move that we appoint a committee of three to find a solution." There was a moment of silence until he added, "After all, too many cooks spoil the broth." With that timely quote, heads began to nod, and soon thereafter the motion was carried.

People are quick to accept an old cliché as words of wisdom passed down by our ancestors. In fact, they often act as if it's heresy to reject its guidance. Undoubtedly the right quote at the right time has provided a solution for many otherwise unsolvable problems.

Interestingly, some of these revered quotations contradict still others. For instance, one that rebuts the above quote is "Two heads are better than one." Or how about "A stitch in time saves nine" or "Don't put off to tomorrow what you can do today" when trying to provoke a prompt decision? These are good ones to promote quick action, that is, unless somebody else says, "Haste makes waste."

I think it's a smart move to memorize several of these "right" quotes so you can be prepared with the appropriate one to fit your side of a heated debate. Frankly, I'm always amazed at the power of a quote to sway people's thinking.

## —NUMBER 10—
### A Sure Way to Make a Poor First Impression

Show up late for an appointment, and I guarantee that you'll make a poor first impression. Other than a bad accident that prevents you from making a telephone call in advance, no excuse for tardiness is acceptable. If the unavoidable happens, you must call, explain, and do your best to apologize profusely. People understand that delays can happen. But being late and failing to call is the epitome of unprofessionalism. It's downright rude. It signals a message, "Since I don't have any respect for your time, I obviously don't respect you either." I can't imagine a worse circumstance under which to meet somebody for the first time.

## —NUMBER 11—
### You Can't Stand Still—
### You Either Go Forward or Backward

Perhaps the Red Queen said it best in Lewis Carroll's *Through the Looking-Glass* when she advised Alice, "Now, *here*, you see, it takes all the running *you* can do, to keep in the same place. If you want to get somewhere else, you must run at least twice as fast." While Carroll probably didn't have today's entrepreneur in mind, his words are well advised. No business can remain stationary. In today's fiercely competitive world, standing still is the same as going backward. If you don't go forward, others will speed right past you.

## —NUMBER 12—
### Doing Business via Long-Distance

It's not uncommon for out-of-town business relationships to break down over a period of time. Perhaps the biggest stumbling block is poor communication—or lack of communication. There's no substitute for eyeball-to-eyeball contact, but when long distances don't permit regular in-person meetings, use the telephone. In fact, use it more frequently than you'd otherwise contact a local person you regularly stop by to visit.

It's amazing how many misunderstandings occur when people have no communication. "But how can that be?" you may ask yourself. "I don't know what she's upset about. I haven't even spoken to her for nine weeks!"

With customers, don't wait until a problem occurs to call. Constantly communicate with them—call to deliver any information you even think they should know. "I just called to let you know the quarterly earnings on XYZ Company are slightly down from what was estimated." "The delivery of your merchandise is running ten to twelve days behind." "I've got some good news to tell you. We received your results from the lab, and you passed your physical examination with flying colors."

If you don't have some pertinent information to discuss with a customer, just call to let the customer know that everything is going smoothly at your end and that you called to find out what's happening at his or her end. The more you keep in touch with somebody, the stronger your relationship grows. It's failing to communicate that causes a relationship to deteriorate.

## —NUMBER 13—
### The Lawn Mower/Brain Surgeon Theory

When a young brain surgeon first begins his or her practice, the odds are slim that the neighbor whose lawn the surgeon used to mow will go to him or her for an operation. The neighbor still thinks of this bright and talented young doctor as the kid with braces who used to cut the grass—and the one who once broke the garage windows. To rephrase a biblical quote, a man is not a prophet in his own home town. A more recent quote is "The expert is the guy from the next town." My theory is based on how a person is remembered by how that person was way back when.

If you accept this theory, you'll know better than to ask your friends and relatives for their opinions about a new business venture you're considering. When UCC was only in the idea stage, I received virtually no support from close acquaintances. To them, I was not what they'd call a merchandising genius. I am certain that if a stranger from afar had the same concept, they would have been more receptive.

Based on this theory, when you begin your career as an insurance agent, an attorney, an architect, computer rep, or whatever, don't anticipate having your friends lining up on your doorstep to do business with you. In time, they will come around, but only *after* you have an established reputation. By then, they will see you for what you are today—with your present identity.

## —NUMBER 14—
### The Dangers of Computer Clutter

One of the big selling points of a computer is that it eliminates paperwork. It's true; volumes of information can be stored on disks. What has happened, however, is that now people have gone overboard on the way they use these extraordinary machines. People collect too much information. For example, someone fires out a request: "Give me a printout of our average customer. I want the demographics on everyone between eighteen and twenty-five—how many parents does he or she have, his or her age, is he or she married, etc."

While there are circumstances where it is useful to review this sort of information, there is a limit to how many times you need to obtain such data. Too often, however, once the computer is programmed, the same printout with updated data is routinely distributed throughout the company every week or month. Once it is in the system, the organization seems incapable of surviving without it. Eventually, the purpose that it originally served has disappeared, and although nobody requests it, the paper doesn't stop coming in.

Nowadays, when you walk into a typical executive's office, it's common to see computer clutter piled so high in every nook and cranny that it's difficult for the executive to function in an organized fashion. Computers are here to stay, and in today's business world, few can operate without them. So what can be done about the clutter? First, discipline yourself to throw away all printouts that are dated or unnecessary. Second, when data is no longer needed, instruct the person in charge of the computer department to stop distributing it.

## —NUMBER 15—
## The Difference Between a Conversation and a Presentation

It doesn't matter what you sell, you should either sell it or don't even attempt to talk about it. In the early stages of UCC, I'd meet somebody at a dinner party, the club, or on the golf course, and they'd ask me to fill them in on what I was doing. Many of these people were good candidates to be club members and even franchisees. And since I was overly anxious to talk about my business, I gave them a condensed version of an actual presentation. It was an explanation in bits and pieces, and no wonder it didn't turn them on—I short-changed them.

What should I have done differently? I should have said, "Look, John, I don't like to mix business with pleasure, and this is not the time to talk shop. I'd be delighted, however, to give you a call on Monday morning, and we'll set up a time to get together." Every salesperson should follow this advice. Never give a partial presentation, because when you do, it's so watered down, it's unlikely that it will be effective. Instead, you want to present your ideas under the most favorable conditions. Believe me, it makes a big difference.

## —NUMBER 16—
## Don't Let Anyone Do Your Selling for You

Following a sales presentation, a salesperson might be told, "It sounds good. I'd like to run it by my partner (spouse, accountant, lawyer, etc.), and I'll get back with you. I'm all for it, but as a matter of protocol, I have to clear it with her first." I'm sure many people who say this really do have good intentions. But every experienced salesperson knows such sales rarely materialize.

There is a combination of reasons why they don't. First, the law of diminishing returns sets in—prospects cool off because they don't remember all of the benefits of your product, but they do remember how much it costs. Second, do you remember the effort you put into learning to give an effective sales presentation? And you were trained to do it. How can you expect somebody who has never been trained to give a good sales presentation on his first attempt? You can't! Third, the prospect will engage in a conversation; he or she will not give a presentation.

So what should you do? You should explain to the prospect, "John, I am an expert in my field. It took a long time for me to develop my expertise. There's a strong chance your partner (spouse, etc.) will ask questions that you won't be able to answer properly. I am sorry, but I can't permit you to do my job for me. However, I will be happy to go with you, and the three of us will sit down, and I'll give that person a full presentation just as I have done for you."

Note that it's important for the first party to be present and listen once more to a complete presentation. Why? Because, if not, he or she may cool off. (Again, the law of diminishing returns will set in.) Before you begin the presentation, you should say something such as, "John has agreed to buy, but before he consents, I have agreed to run this by you." This starts matters off on a positive note.

## —NUMBER 17—
### The Negative Sell

Here is one of the best selling techniques in the book. Simply put, after you've presented your product, you tell the prospect why it might *not* be good for him or her. Or, for that matter, why the prospect can't or shouldn't get it. And then you let the prospect tell you why it is good for him or her and why he or she should buy.

For example, after I have explained the benefits of a UCC membership, I say, "But, of course, both of you are in your fifties, and now that you're successful, you own two homes, and have so much, you might not feel a need to save thousands of dollars a year as a club member." This opens the door for the prospect to reply, "We're not so affluent that we no longer want a good deal. Besides, there are still many things we'll be purchasing over the next ten years. We will have to replace some of our furniture, our stereo, watches, and who knows what else." Do you see what I'm doing? I'm letting the prospect sell me on why he or she should buy.

The same technique works with a prospective franchisee. "This opportunity might not be for you. It involves long hours, and it's hard work. It's definitely not for everyone. It takes a special individual to be suited for our business. Of course, those who qualify can enjoy exceptionally high incomes."

"I'm not afraid of hard work," is the general response, "and this is exactly the kind of opportunity I've been looking for."

When I sold oil well investments, after my sales presentation, I'd say, "Bob, you've only been a dentist for seven years, so perhaps when you're more established, say, in fifteen years, you might be in a position to handle an investment such as this."

"I've got some apartment buildings and some other interests," the dentist would answer. "I think I can swing one of these deals."

Using the negative sell, a real estate agent says, "This home might be too expensive for you. Bear in mind, your mortgage payments will be 30 percent more than with your previous home."

"I understand," the prospect replies. "But my income has more than doubled since we purchased our present home."

The negative sell is applicable in every field. It works, but only when you use it with sincerity. Otherwise, it comes across as phony and too high-pressure.

## —NUMBER 18—
### Different Strokes for Different Folks

Every year during income tax season, my CPA sits down with me and asks me what seem like hundreds of questions: "When did you sell this stock?" "Were there any dividends?" "Was this expense business or personal?" "What do you estimate your charitable contributions were this year compared with last year's?"

Once, in a fit of frustration, I said to him, "It would drive me crazy if I had to deal with the numbers and details that you handle."

"That's interesting," he replied, "because I always thought it would drive me nuts if I were you and had to run your business."

I thought for a moment and commented, "I guess it's a good thing everybody is different. It would be a boring world if we were all identical."

It's a serious mistake to lump all people together and treat them identically. While there are certain common denominators about everyone, no two people are identical. The effective manager knows how to read people and, accordingly, reacts to different personalities. Such a manager also realizes that everyone has an ego, but egos come in a variety of sizes. Some need more attention than others—but every ego responds well to some encouragement. This is even true with the person who says, "I never let my ego get in the way." Perhaps it is especially true with this individual. It is also essential to understand that having an ego and being egotistical are not the same.

I recently read an interesting interview of Ford Motor Co.'s past CEO, Donald Petersen, conducted with a group of reporters at a farewell breakfast meeting upon his retirement. Petersen talked about his friends "Roger and Lee" (GM's CEO Roger Smith, and Chrysler's CEO Lee Iacocca):

> We are all products of World War II as young adults, and we are also products of a period of dominant American industrial might, during which there was also dominant American automotive might. [But] we are all dramatically different people, and it suggests that there is no "formula" [for choosing the right chief executive]. Lee was the most obvious among us, who as a young person, was seen as someone who might rise to one of these positions. Lee is one of the few people who could have gone to Chrysler and do what he did there. Roger is very much a product of the GM system, a very logical outgrowth of the GM way. I'm probably the biggest surprise of the bunch.

## —NUMBER 19—
### Understand Your Limitations

There's a tendency for a person who succeeds in one area to think he or she can do anything. While self-confidence is a positive attribute, it can be carried too far. Unless there is a strong correlation, success doesn't necessarily carry over from one field to another. This is particularly true in today's competitive business world—an era in which the specialist carves his or her own little niche. Even General Motors, the world's largest industrial corporation, now knows better than to attempt to make a car for every buyer.

How many times have you seen a group of doctors, accountants, and lawyers open a restaurant? While statistics show an incredibly high turnover in the retail food business, I've witnessed dozens of successful professional people lose their shirts in such ventures. The restaurant business is a difficult field. What criteria do these people have who think they're so smart that they can succeed in a highly competitive field that has nothing in common with their own livelihoods? The only criterion I can observe is that they each have their own personal food tastes—hardly a reason to invest in a business.

Managers who understand their own limitations are smart enough to delegate to people they believe are smarter than they in their respective fields. Again, a good manager doesn't allow his or her ego to get in the way.

## —NUMBER 20—
### Keep Physically Fit

Physical fitness is a subject you expect to find in a book about health or beauty awareness. But I think it's a subject that also has a lot of merit in the world of business for several reasons. First and most obvious, physically fit people are sick less often and have fewer days absent from work. Second, when you look good and feel good, you have a better self-image. Third, the better shape you're in, the more stamina you have. Sometimes, during the course of a long, drawn out meeting, the person who wears down first loses. Having that extra burst of energy can be a real advantage. Fourth, keeping physically fit is an excellent discipline, which you can carry over to your career. When you are trim and fit, it also signals to others that you are disciplined. Fifth, the brain functions best when it is housed in a strong, healthy body.

## —NUMBER 21—
## A Touch of Humor

In practically every situation, I've been able to find a place for humor in business, although some people act as if it's never appropriate. Frankly, I think humor relaxes people. It's a mistake when you take yourself too seriously. It's good to be able to step back and laugh at yourself. What's more, humor makes business more fun. And certainly everyone should enjoy his or her work.

Naturally, there are many different kinds of humor. The only kind I don't like is the kind that's hurtful and generates a laugh at somebody else's expense. In particular, I like humor when a person makes him- or herself the butt of the joke. I'll frequently do this, and it serves as a good icebreaker. It helps develop rapport with people. They tend to take a person who can laugh at him- or herself as nonthreatening. At other times, this form of humor makes others feel more comfortable. For instance, blind or obese people might make jokes about themselves to put others at ease. In doing this, they demonstrate that they're really no different from any other person.

I also make myself the scapegoat of a joke to get a message across. For example, I might tell a secretary who is constantly misspelling words in my correspondence, "I'd say you're the worst speller in the world, but that wouldn't be true. I am. But keep it up, and you're going to get my crown. Now, I want you to make me look good, so would you please place the dictionary next to you, and when in doubt, check for spelling errors. Or better yet, use the computer to check for errors."

A common request these days is: "Do you mind if I smoke?" As a nonsmoker, I can't stand cigarette smoke, and I'm sure a majority of nonsmokers feel the same way. So, naturally, I mind. But instead of hurting somebody's feelings by saying, "Yes, and don't you dare smoke around me," I reply, "You know, the one thing I enjoy most in life is ashes all over me, and I love the smell of smoke on my clothes. But in particular, I love to inhale secondary smoke even though I don't get the enjoyment from it as does the actual smoker. Still, I want my lungs to take in as much as possible."

Humor can also open doors. When I call somebody on the phone and a secretary asks about the nature of my call, I'll say something like, "Please tell Mr. Jones that I'm at his house now with a truckload of pork bellies that he purchased in the commodities market. I want to find out if they belong in the basement or on the front lawn."

Or if the secretary asks, "Does he know you?" I reply, "No, but I'm from his insurance company, and I wanted to let him know that the fire has been put out, and the only real structural damage appears to be the roof."

And my favorite is when a secretary asks if the boss knows the reason for my call. I reply, "No, not unless he is a mind reader."

## —NUMBER 22—
### And This Too Shall Pass

There's an old fable about a powerful emperor who assembled all of his wisest men and gave them an ultimatum: "You have thirty days to deliver to me a single, concise sentence that I can use to serve as a solution to every problem brought to me. Do it, and you shall be richly rewarded. If you fail, you shall be beheaded."

While I will spare the details of the story, these wise men came up with the line, "And this too shall pass." These are indeed wise words. No matter how upsetting a crisis may be at the moment, "And this too shall pass" is applicable. It's a wonderful thought that generally puts things in a proper prospective.

## —NUMBER 23—
### Think Globally

For those who haven't already observed, the wave of the future is a worldwide marketplace. Just a few decades ago,

American entrepreneurs thought in terms of cities, counties, and states when determining where their goods were sold. Marketing areas now have no boundaries. Global expansion adds a whole new dimension, one that is challenging and guaranteed to be more demanding. No longer can American businesspeople bury their heads in the sand and only think domestically.

Instead, we must look at the opportunities that lie ahead around the world. We are living in exciting times. Even small entrepreneurs must think globally; while the business is still in its infancy, one eye should focus on the present, and the other on the future. Accordingly, the direction taken during the business's first steps will in time leave a footprint in faraway lands.

## —NUMBER 24—
## America: The Land of Opportunity

Even our multinational corporations such as AT&T, Coca-Cola, Exxon, Ford, and IBM, which have spread their operations across the globe, have no single marketplace that compares to total sales generated in the United States. So while corporate America expands abroad, and as foreign companies fiercely compete to get a foothold in our country, we must never forget that this is still the greatest land of opportunity in the history of civilization.

While it is true that America does not dominate the world economy as we did during the 1950s and early 1960s, we are still the envy of every nation, bar none. We are blessed with exceptional national resources, a strong work ethic, and a democracy that promotes individual freedom. For those who seek the attainment of the American dream, it still exists and is available to all. I know because I experienced it beyond my wildest dreams. May you too realize yours. I can think of no more appropriate way in which to end this book than by saying, "God bless America."